Table of Contents

View of Delft, 1660–61 by Johannes Vermeer

Editor

I have too many friends. Why am I saying such a thing? I don't have the time to visit all of them.

How many friends are enough? The January Economist had a piece about a study to gauge the impact of Facebook and the likes of that monster. They had two categories. One was what I would call acquaintances that you like. The statistical average is 155. I still have the list of contacts from work in 1999, which included some people not associated with the phone business. It has 157 names on it with their addresses and phone numbers. For once, I'm typical. The sample singled out the younger Facebook crowd and it was 187. I expected a much larger number.

The second category was close friends that you call or visit at least twice a year. That statistical number was fifteen. Twelve for the Facebook bunch. This is where I'm off the norm by quite a bit. I meet for lunch with a group of about twelve every Tuesday. Then there are four retired co-workers living five minutes away. We meet about twice a month. My immediate families are friends. Counting brother, sister, and their offspring adds twenty. We get together several times a year. I have fifty-four cousins on both sides of my family. We still have reunions in June that have been going on at least since I was a toddler. Last year the total was about 60 Alston descendants.

Almost forgot about church. I am a member of a very supportive church. A few weeks ago, I had an emergency visit to the hospital. Thanks to smart phone email, member prayers had been dispatched to Heaven before I got checked in. That is real friendship!

Then there are my distant friends who are not family that I used to visit a couple of times a year. Three live in Southwest Virginia, where I was District Manager in the 1970s. I would visit them every week if I could. One now lives in Panama. Ed Short, a man who knows everything, lives in Wichita, Kansas. This group includes people in several walks of life, a wide range of personalities, lifetime achievements, education levels. Some have high intellect and education, my brother is one of them. One is a black farmer who has enough common sense on farming to match my brother. He and I quail hunted together for over 40 years. He was a peerless wing shot in 33 eastern North Carolina counties. I would visit all of them every week if I could.

You may be wondering what kind of people these friends are. None of these folks and I have ever had a disagreement to the point of raised voices, unless it was funny.

If it were possible, there are a few more that I would like to add to my friends list. On top of this list is historian Will Durant who wrote the eleven-volume *Story of Civilization* and *The Story of Philosophy*. Michael Grant, who wrote histories of the Etruscans, Greeks, and Romans. Another would be C. S. Lewis, Christian theologian and moralist, and St. Jerome, who God put in charge of developing the Bible. He set a high standard as far as public relations. Jesus' name in Hebrew is Joshua. Joshua was the Jim Smith name among the Hebrews at the time. I read somewhere in the Old Testament about a father who named all seven of his sons Joshua. By choosing the Greek version, Jesus' name became unique and a PR success that will never be equaled. St. Jerome did the same thing with the Apostle Paul, whose Jewish name was Saul, another very popular Hebrew name.

Johannes Kepler, a German mathematician and astronomer (1571-1630) who developed fascinating theories on planetary movements and time travel. He reminds me of me because he never considered any idea to be impossible. I also share his lack of sentimentality about "beliefs" and trust numbers more than words. Knowing and believing are two very different concepts in any operational sense.

Roman Emperor Marcus Aurelius, who wrote *Meditations* between battles on the Roman frontier. Father Thomas Merton, who wrote *The Seven Storey Mountain*.

This could go on and on, but you get the idea. If Kepler was right in his theoretical calculations, meeting with friends in Heaven will be infinitely easier. He theorized that, since Heaven is eternal and, outside temporal time, everything happens at once. Following that to its logical conclusion leads us to accept that the physical universe is a figment of God's imagination. The Bible says we were created in God's image. Jesus said if we believed, we could do anything He could do.

The Bible uses different references to our relationship to God. When in reference to our temporal existence, God "Holds us in His hands" or "Is with us." When in reference to our spiritual existence, it is "In Him." This is not style, nor is it translation carelessness. It is deliberate. There is a big difference between "with" and "in." "With" conjures up images like me in a big conference room with all the other saved souls with God at the head table planning something really, really good, and we are "helping" Him make His decision.

Not so. "In" means "part of." Both Aquinas and Augustine wrote long, tedious, pieces about this to explain that Heaven was God. Milton has several stanzas in *Paradise Lost* on the subject. C. S. Lewis uses it in *The Lion, the Witch and the Wardrobe*. So, Kepler's theories confirm the work of the greatest Christian thinkers who have ever lived.

Where are we now? Upon achieving Heaven, our reality becomes our ideas. Within the two known universes, and all the other possible universes, there is none other like me, or like you. As the Face Book crowd would say, AWESOME!

Gene Alston

A Surprising Bargain
Sybil Austin Skakle

My father, Andrew Shanklin Austin, Sr., a merchant for over fifty years in Hatteras Village, learned a lot about reality and human nature during that time. A poem in a handmade wooden frame, hanging beside the store office door, spoke of the idealistic hope that men might meet and trust one another. The beginning words said, "If I knew you and you knew me, 'Tis seldom we would disagree ..."

Stores at Hatteras were gathering places back in the twenties and thirties. Daddy kept the store open to catch last minute trade and late opinions. Such good conversation went on around the stove in the wintertime! In the summer, the same location drew the usual crowd to sit on two handcrafted benches and exchange views, or get into some heated discussion.

Sometimes when things were slow, or someone else waited on the trade, Daddy could be found by his old oak, roll top desk, which had been part of the salvage of the Schooner Carroll A. Deering, shipwrecked off Hatteras January 31, 1921. Daddy was catching up on things in the store office. One Saturday evening, a man of the community came into his office to ask about opening an account. Most folks let accounts run from month to month and came in once a month to "settle up." Daddy knew this man well and asked him, "Haven't you been trading with Dolph Burrus?"

"Yes, sir, I have."

Daddy didn't beat around the bush, nor waste his time, nor the man's. He came right to the point. "Has Dolph turned you away because you haven't been paying your bills?"

Probably embarrassed by that, the said man must have been astonished when Daddy continued. "If I take you on and you don't pay me, I'll have to turn you away. I think the best thing for me to do for both of us is this."

Daddy shifted on his right hip in the oak, swivel desk chair, reached into the pocket of his pants with his left hand. He handed the man a ten-dollar bill, at a time when ten dollars would buy an ample supply of groceries for a family for a week.

Perhaps the man thanked him. Maybe not.

Telling Mama about it later, Daddy laughed hilariously. Laughter for Daddy came rarely. When he laughed, his eyes crinkled with amusement and his breaths came with quick gasping sounds in his throat. He was so amused he could hardly finish his story.

"Do you know what he did?" Tears filled his eyes. He laughed again. "He took the ten dollars I'd given him and walked out of my store to spend it somewhere else."

No, Daddy did not suspect the man would spend it on other than groceries. The cause for his amusement was the joke on himself that he saw in the happening.

Finally sober, he pondered the matter for a moment. Then he chuckled a little and said, "It was a bargain for all that! I saved myself a lot of worry."

The story was originally in *Confessions of an Outer Banks Filly* as *Hatteras Merchant*.

Appetite for Mulberries
(Learning about silk on a trip to Turkey)

Joan Leotta

At the carpet factory
our guide displayed
tiny tightly wound balls,
balls for a Doll-sized tennis court,
actually cocoons
left by the little worms
who had feasted on mulberry leaves.

The threads from their post-prandial weaving
were boiled, then separated and dyed
for the carpets of a Sultan's court.
The shrouding is offered to us
in woven carpets far
beyond my budget

On leaving, I salute the tiny weavers
Who gave their lives for silken
Splendor.
I too share their appetite for mulberries
though it is the berries,
not the leaves that I devour.
At breakfast
I add a handful of

deep purple berries to my cereal
and rejoice that the berries had no
value to Sultans then or now.

Republican Presidential Debates
E. B. Alston

Moderator: What will you do about the Antarctic penguins if the South Pole shifts to Filthy McNasty's Bar and Grill in Fort Worth, Texas?

Donald Trump: My wall, that the Mexicans paid for, will control penguin immigration. If any unwanted penguins slip through, I will fly them back to Antarctica and make the Paraguayans pay for it.

Ted Cruz: If the people of the United States elect me president, I will deal with this just like I would deal with everything else. It will be in accord with the Constitution and scientific precepts contained in the King James Bible.

Voice from the Crowd: What about the penguins?

Ted Cruz: Texas is hotter than Antarctica, especially in summer, so the South Pole temperature might be, let's say, -15 1/2°. I don't believe the penguins would be inconvenienced. As for what I would, and will do as soon as this debate is over, is send an emergency email to every email address in the United States requesting that my constituents cough up more cash quickly before the forces of darkness overwhelm my campaign for the presidency.

Marco Rubio: There you go again, Ted! It's -15 8/16°! You distort the facts with every word out of your mouth. As for myself, I will treat the penguins with respect and honor their wishes if they wish to stay in Texas.

Voice from the Crowd: How will the penguins deal with the bull scrotum ashtrays at Filthy McNasty's?

Marco Rubio: They must accept Americans as we are. Plus, I'm sure the customers at Filthy McNasty's will make adjustments.

Another Voice from the Crowd: The penguins; are you just gonna let 'em walk right in? We got too many greedy, lazy, foreigners on the tab now.

Marco Rubio: I will not allow our borders to be sieves. I will protect the sanctity of America's borders. I will guard our financial resources. I will make our country safe and secure. In every imaginable way, I will do a better job than Ted Cruz. (Long pause.) And furthermore, I will not allow our borders to be sieves. I will protect the sanctity of America's borders. I will guard our financial resources. I will make our country safe and secure. And I will treat the penguins with respect and honor their wishes if they wish to stay in Texas. And then, I will treat the penguins with respect and honor their wishes if they wish to stay in Texas. I will not allow our borders to be sieves. I will protect the sanctity of America's borders. I will guard our financial resources. I will make our country safe and secure.

Carly Fiorina: My operational experience in business makes me uniquely prepared to deal with situations such as this. When I was named president of Lucent Technologies after it split off from AT&T Network, I realized that Lucent would not succeed on its own without stringent labor cost controls. We had 135,000 workers spread all over the globe. In three years I cut the force to under 35,000 but I kept the headquarters staff up to allow us to manage operations more efficiently. If you choose me to be your next president, I will deal with every circumstance AND cut government expense.

Another Voice from the Crowd: Ain't LooseScent Technologies gone to be with some French company now?

Carly Fiorina: Well, yes. We had to turn down projects because we didn't have the workers to do the jobs. The company was losing money.

Jeb Bush: (To himself.) I cannot believe this! Cruz and Rubio can't manage themselves in a 12-person debate and they think they can run a country?

Voice from the Crowd: Hey, little Bush Bro. You gonna tell us how you is gonna fix anything?

Jeb Bush: I am a pragmatic man with executive experience. My record as Governor of Florida speaks for itself. My administration initiated changes that made state government more efficient in serving Florida citizens and, at the same time, reduced both costs and taxes.

Voice from the Crowd: What about the penguins? What if the South Pole shifted to Miami?

Jeb Bush: (Laughed) I was not, and am not, worried about the South Pole shifting anywhere. It has been where it is for millions of years. We have more immediate concerns to deal with in order to get this great country back on track.

Another Voice from the Crowd: Aw, he's just Dub Ya's little bro. We ain't got to pay him no mind.

Another Voice from the Crowd: Right. He ain't never been nothing but governor of Florida. He ain't ready for the big 'un yet.

Another Voice from the Crowd: I'm wid Rubio and Cruz. They know's stuff none of them big lawyer city slickers knows.

Another Voice from the Crowd: Yeah. They knows a lot of stuff.

Voice from the Crowd: Who you gonna vote for?

Another Voice from the Crowd: Trump.

Voice from the Crowd: Why? He's a New York City slicker Yankee.

Voice from the Crowd: He's the only one that answered the question.

Another Voice from the Crowd: I think I will, too, 'cause his wife is real pretty.

Life With Elizabeth
"It Ain't Your Grandpa's Post Office Anymore"
Elizabeth Silance Ballard

I made one of my fairly frequent treks to the post office today to buy stamps and to mail a manila envelope with two newspapers in it. I am of the age, now, that I compare everything to the way "it used to be." Yes, I know this is a sign of aging but I don't care because, of course, I'm right about it all: Nothing is as good as it used to be but everything costs umpteen times more than it did "back then."

Back then, it cost two cents to mail a letter (compared to today's cost) and a stamped post card was one cent. (God only know how much it costs, now.) Back then, the nice man in the cage behind the iron bars told us what our total charges were, smiled as he said it, commented on our beauty or the weather, and that was that. I guess he could smile because he felt safe. None of us could leap over the counter, pry open the bars, and choke the living daylights out of him, which brings us to my experience at the P.O. in this day and time.

Today, for instance, after a very lengthy wait in a very long line, I finally made it to the front of that line and was summoned to the counter where there was only one clerk on duty even though there were four workstations at the counter. I handed him my manila envelope and he started: Was there anything perishable, dangerous, etc." You know the spiel. I assured him the package was completely harmless. No gas cans, no bombs, no weapons of any kind, no Obama cartoons.

Then he started in on the 47 different ways the envelope could be mailed. Did I want the super duper service, which would cost $18 and give me $100 worth of insurance on the package? Did I want the next in line service, which was a guaranteed delivery of 3-4 days? Did I want Certified Mail? Registered Mail? Delivery confirmation? Did I want insurance, which I could get even though I didn't take the super duper service package? I had already told him the manila envelope contained only two newspapers, so I proceeded to refuse all his offerings and opt for the cheapo mail service, which was still $1.90 to travel roughly an hour and a half in a truck with hundreds, perhaps even thousands, of other pieces of mail. He made no comment.

Did I need stamps, envelopes, mailing boxes, etc.? Yes, that spiel. No, I only needed 100 stamps. Did I want the—and he named off all the different artwork stamps in his drawer, I guess. I advised him I just needed a roll of stamps after which he started counting out strips of a few stamps to a page. I made no comment.

As I approached my driveway, my mail lady was driving away. Yes, we still get once a day delivery in this country, at least here in Richmond County; but in Onslow County (city of Jacksonville, to be precise) back in the 1950s, our mail man made two deliveries a day. Yes, even on Saturday. He came on holidays, too. In fact, I distinctly remember him coming on Sunday during the Christmas holidays because, of course, everyone got loads of Christmas cards. He came in all sorts of weather and he was always whistling, smiling and spoke a few words to whichever one of us met him at the door to get the mail.

Now, I'm not an MBA graduate of some prestigious university, but it seems to me that if the postal service would stop commissioning various artists to come up with special artwork stamps, postage might, could, possibly be lowered! Yes, I say l-o-w-e-r-e-d—that word and concept so hated by the U.S. Government.

Folks, do you REALLY CARE whose photo is on your stamps? Is it really vital to have stamps featuring Mickey Mouse, Elvis Presley, and the like gracing your checks to the utility companies? Your car payment? Your house payment? Stamps are a tax, people! Not a status symbol!

Other countries do not appear to have such a variety to choose from and most often have only the photo of their country's leader. Queen Elizabeth II, for instance. I say that we shouldn't even have that! Stick to something really patriotic such as the flag and let all the rest of it go! Oh, I know there has to be some change when they raise the price of stamps again but stick to something simple. Stick to something they already have the dies for and not pay for new ones to be drawn and painted like a portrait! They wouldn't have to raise prices so frequently.

Yes, the post offices used to sell postage and deliver the mail in a timely fashion for a minimum of cost. About the only other things in the building were the "Wanted" posters on the wall. But now? Well, our government agency is now in the retail business selling boxes, bubble wrap, address stickers, packages, and I don't know what all!

Not only are they in the retail business, they have now entered the rat race of advertising. Yes, folks, think about it. Our postal service pays to advertise all those products and their services. On television, even! Why? Are they afraid UPS and others will take away some of their business? Why are they competing?

I would really like to know how much the postal service would save if they cut out all the advertising and all the artists they employ and use some common sense. All we need is something that will enable to post office to deliver our mail. Come to think of it, they don't need to commission stamp artists, or pay for the cost of printing new stamps at all. Just a man with a stamper and a big inkpad would do just fine. He collects whatever the current cost is, slams down the stamper proclaiming to one and all that the citizen has "PAID" to have this piece of mail delivered! Problem and massive costs issue solved.

"He listens well who takes notes." Dante

"If in other sciences we should arrive at certainty without doubt and truth without error, it behooves us to place the foundation of knowledge in mathematics." Roger Bacon

A Day in the Gun Shop
Tim Whealton

Maybe you think it would be fun to own your own business. A lot of people tell me having your own business is wonderful. They tell me you can set your own hours, work when you want, and do everything at your own pace. I knew better before I started but I didn't know how interesting it would be working with the public! You just never know what is going to walk through that door!

It was 6:30 am and a man came in looking a little weak. He sits and asks if I have a blood pressure cuff. I say yes but then ask why do you want your BP checked at a gun shop at 06:30? He says he has chest pain but doesn't want to go to the ER and put up with all those tests. I try my best to convince him to let me call 911 but he refuses. I even have an old EKG machine and print out an EKG. It shows abnormalities but I still can't get him to go. Later the pain gets worse and his wife takes him to the ER. Doctor says his EKG shows abnormalities and he needs to go to the heart unit. He tells the doctor his gunsmith told him that at no charge. Doctor calls me to find out if I'm a doctor. I end up explaining and doctor brings out two pistols for trigger work.

Another day a man comes in early and asks if we are alone. He just got a call his wife was having an affair with another man. When he asked the woman why she was calling to tell on her, she said she was seeing her too and cheating on her. He said he needed to talk to somebody and dropped off a rifle for cleaning and sight in. I had to make sure he was planning on using it to hunt deer instead of Dear!

Charlie comes in and asked me help to catch some cows that are out. They are in town in Cove City and running behind the houses. There are 6 cows each over 1000 pounds. I developed a new found appreciation for cowboys.

A mother brings in her daughter that has pushed an earring up her nose and can't get it out. I can see it with my bore scope but I don't try to remove it because she might aspirate it into her lung. I sent that one to the doctor! The mother tells others about my flexible bore scope and local people come in to look in their ears and noses. One asks if she can take it home overnight, but I don't loan tools.

A man comes in and was waiting to talk about his rifle. He is looking at a calendar and is upset from looking at a picture of a B-52 Bomber. He explains that he was in Vietnam and his small unit was almost wiped out by a force of 6000 North Vietnamese troops. They happened to be in front of this force that was headed to attack a Special Forces base. It was sunset and there was no way to evacuate. They were given all available ammo and instructed to dig in. Their officers came by and thanked them and said it was an honor to serve with them. They expected enemy contact shortly after midnight. When the enemy was less than one mile a huge flight of B-52 bombers were rerouted from a mission to bomb North Vietnam and they started pounding the enemy force. The enemy force was stopped and forced to dig in. They evacuated his company at daylight with helicopters and he came home two weeks later. He didn't know why but all these events had come back to haunt him in dreams over 40 years later.

The town drunk comes in extremely intoxicated at quitting time. I feed him some soup and take him home in my truck. I come back to the shop the next morning and find his false teeth on the table.

Two men come in with a woman. They are huge and barefooted. They have heard that my wife passed away and they have brought me their sister. They tell me she can cook and skin game better than a man. She doesn't talk but smiles and she is missing more than one tooth. I look around for the hidden camera but there isn't one.

Maybe because I'm a little unconventional, I attract situations or maybe it's because I'm a one person business. Don't know for sure but it sure is interesting.

I Sailed on the SS United States
Rita Berman

She was known as the fastest ocean liner ever built. On her maiden voyage in 1952, the SS United States received the Blue Riband for the Trans-Atlantic speed record. I strolled her decks more than sixty years ago, on September 16, 1955, when I sailed from New York to Southampton on this magnificent vessel that was longer than the Titanic. Designed by naval architect William Francis Gibbs of Philadelphia and built in Newport News, VA, with steel from the Lukens Company in Coatesville, she became a symbol of America's post-war innovation.

I was returning home to England after spending a year in the United States, living in Jenkintown, Pennsylvania, and working as a secretary for a sales engineer.

I had gone to the United States at the invitation of an American professor from Beaver College, whom I met on a bus tour in England visiting a stately home. We sat next to each other on the bus and chatted. The following day I went on a different trip to another location, but here again I found myself next to Mrs. Mackinnon and we continued our conversation. The result was that Mrs. Mackinnon sponsored me so that I could stay with her and get a job. It took me a year to get a "green card." I had to go to the American Embassy in Grosvenor Square, London, complete an application, and be interviewed. I was asked such questions as "was I or had I been a member of the Communist Party?" and "did I intend to engage in prostitution while in the United States?" Years later, when I applied for American citizenship in Greensboro, NC, I was asked the same two questions. Again my response was "No." A friend of mine had to accompany me to Greensboro to personally vouch that she knew me.

On my first voyage to the United States, I had sailed on the SS. Maasdam to New York and arrived September 1954. I was only 22 years old. Mrs. Mackinnon met me at the port and drove me to her home in her new Chevrolet. It was a very large car by English standards. Her god-daughter was attending Beaver College and also lived with us. The office where I worked was in an old coach house, and had no air-conditioning. I was surprised to see my boss come to work in Bermuda shorts.

After saving up more than a thousand dollars, which was pretty good considering that I was only earning about $40 a week, I felt it was time to return home. By coincidence, a friend of mine, Yvonne Hope, had been working in Canada during the same period. When we discovered we were sailing on the same crossing for the SS United States, her father who was an official with the Pacific and Orient Lines arranged for us to have our cabin upgraded to the first-class section, but we still had to eat in the tourist class. My memoir from that time records that we had fun on board flirting with the unattached men. The ship was large and well stabilized and it took on five days to cross the ocean. I was not seasick then, but had been on the SS. Maasdam. We were well care for by our steward. On the first day, he brought us caviar and crackers left over from a party held in first class. It was my first taste of caviar and I was not impressed. I remember that our cabin had beds not bunks.

I still have a copy of the tourist class passenger list as well as photographs of Yvonne and me aboard the ship. It had 2000 passenger beds and a crew of 1,000. What luxury. Other facts were that a haircut in the Beauty Parlor cost $1.25 and a manicure $1.00. For men, the price of a shave was 45 cents and a haircut 90 cents. There was a dress code for the Dining Saloon. Ladies were to "refrain from wearing shorts and gentlemen are requested to wear a coat or jacket."

Back in England, I was unable to settle down. I couldn't get used to the smallness of the cars, houses, and the outdated office equipment. I worked for an import-export agent and was using a manual typewriter and taking dictation in shorthand. Although I persuaded my boss to get an electric typewriter and use a Dictaphone machine, it wasn't enough.

I decided to return to the United States but this time with my younger sister who was also sponsored by Mrs. Mackinnon. We sailed on the TSS New York that took 11 days to cross the ocean, it was a rough crossing and yes I was sea-sick. My mother's cousin met us and drove us to Albany, New York, where her father rented us an apartment. Ann and I worked for Albany Medical College in the same office as medical secretaries. After a few years, we moved to New York City, shared an apartment with two other sisters, and found jobs in the medical field. Later we both met and married Americans.

Last year, a cousin of mine who knew I had sailed on the SS United States, sent me newspaper clippings about the efforts to rescue and restore the ship. I learned that Susan Gibbs, the Executive Director of the SS United States Conservancy, is the granddaughter of William Gibbs, and is spearheading the fund-heading efforts of the Conservancy to advance a redevelopment plan.

From 1952 to 1968, the ship had carried presidents John F. Kennedy, Dwight Eisenhower, and Harry Truman. Bill Clinton sailed on her across the Atlantic to begin his Rhodes scholarship. Marilyn Monroe and Sylvia Plath were also passengers.

The SS United States was taken from service in 1969. In 1996, it was moved from Newport News, VA, to Philadelphia. She has been docked at pier 82, in Philadelphia for 19 years, after years of sales and auctions during which its interior was stripped. The SS United States Conservancy bought it outright in 2011 and since then has been trying to get it restored as a site for a museum and entertainment. It costs $60,000 to $80,000 a month to maintain. Last year, the Conservancy was faced with the ship being sold for scrap, but thousands of supporters around the world have responded with donations.

Washington businessman Jim Pollin sent $120,000 that helped avoid having to sell one of the ship's massive propellers to raise cash. In addition, Pollin matched contributions of another $120,000. Since then thousands of supporters have responded with tax-deductible donations. From Thomas, an eleven-year-old boy in Florida who sent a $5 bill and a drawing of the ship in red, white, and blue magic marker, to former deck officer Richard O'Leary who donated $100,000, and an anonymous donor who contributed $250,000 because it would be "unthinkable to let the SS United States go to the breakers," people are rallying.

The Conservancy is collecting stories from former passengers or anyone who may have a connection to the ship. I sent in my story. This will become part of the Legacy Project archival collection that will be a component of the interactive exhibition in the future SS United States museum.

End

Doomsday Final Exam
Test Your End-Times IQ!!
James Finn Garner
From *Apocalypse Wow! A Memoir for the End of Time*
Slightly modified

What are the names of the Four Horsemen of the Apocalypse?
1. War, Famine, Pestilence, and Death
2. John, Paul, George, and Ringo
3. Plague, Strife, Starvation, and Arsenio
4. Manny, Moe, Jack, and Death

How many rabbis sit in Zurich and control the world's banking activities?
1. Thirteen
2. Four, with seven during peak hours and a half-day on Saturdays for your convenience
3. Only 12; the 13th has to stand because of this pain in his back, which is killing him, oy!
4. Yeah, sure, like they'd let anyone know

What is meant by the term Rapture?
1. The ascension of all true Christians before the beginning of the strife and tribulation caused by the Antichrist
2. The feeling you get when you turn off The 700 Club
3. A new fragrance from Calvin Klein
4. A medical condition that requires a truss

If you are driving on the highway when the Rapture comes, and other drivers are pulled bodily out of theirs vehicle to heaven, what's your best course of action?
1. Pull over to the side of the road until the driver-less traffic stops
2. Look for a nicer make of car than yours, drive alongside, and climb in
3. Speed like hell, because the highway patrol will be too busy to stop you
4. Repent your sins and head for the nearest Stuckey's

The great mystic Nostradamus predicted that the world would end via a
1. "King of Terror" appearing in the sky
2. "Ghost Riders" appearing in the sky
3. Botulism
4. A lack of interest

Many prominent astronomers now admit that the earth will be devastated by a gigantic asteroid, and that this will happen
1. Soon
2. Very soon
3. Extremely soon
4. Today
5. Yesterday

Which of the following should be considered absolutely essential for your bomb shelter provisions?

1. Water purification pills
2. Canned vegetables
3. First-aid kit
4. Yahtzee

One of the basic tenets of the imminent earth changes is the pole shift, which is

1. A radical displacement of the earth's geographic poles from their present position
2. The 8-to-4 workers in a Chicago sausage factory
3. A demographic change in Hamtramck
4. Something baseball players often do in the batter's box

Quartz crystals are a good source of spiritual energy because

1. Their perfectly geometric cellular structure allow* them to receive and store psychic vibrations
2. They make nicer jewelry than D-cell batteries
3. They're safer than sticking a fork in your toaster
4. They're just so shiny and stuff

Who is the Whore of Babylon mentioned in the Book of Revelation?

1. The Pope
2. The antipope
3. Sine'ad O'Connor
4. A certain favorite "advisor" to Saddam Hussein and his buddies

Christian fundamentalists believe the Bible is the literal, unerring word of God because

1. It says so, right there in the Bible
2. Their parents said so
3. They would be so heartbroken if no one ever found Noah's Ark
4. It's easier than thinking

The number of the Beast of the Apocalypse is

1. 666
2. 999
3. Pennsylvania 6-5000
4. Unlisted

The first insight in James Hedfield's *The Celestine Prophecy* is

1. A spiritual awakening is occurring in human culture, brought about by a critical mass of individuals who experience their lives as a spiritual unfolding, a journey in which they are led forward by mysterious circumstances
2. Same as above, plus an emphasis on the health benefits of cooking with hot peppers
3. Hair spray can help remove ink stains on fabric before washing
4. "Hey, this New Age publishing racket isn't so tough after all"

Are the people of the earth reaching a shared consciousness, wherein our converging psychic energy will eliminate strife and lead us into a new golden age?
1. Yes
2. Yes, absolutely
3. Can't argue with that
4. Wow, you know, I can feel it toot

Eleventh-century monk St. Malachy recorded a prophecy of the history of the popes by writing a series of
1. Cryptic mottos for each
2. Dirty limericks for each
3. Funny rebuses for each
4. Bubble-gum cards for each

America's most famous prophet, Edgar Cayce, was known for making his psychic predictions in
1. His sleep
2. His wife's lingerie
3. A high-pitched, sort of Chinese accent
4. Total disregard for the lack of accuracy among his previous prophecies

Nostradamus correctly predicted all of the following except
1. Napoleon's defeat at Waterloo
2. Hitler's invasion of France
3. The assassination of John F. Kennedy
4. The verdict in the 0. J. Simpson trial

The ancient calendar of the Mayans is important for us today because
1. It runs out in the year 2012
2. A new pocket edition is being prepared by Hallmark
3. It adds an important element of multiculturalism to telling time
4. It sure didn't do them a lot of good

The Harmonic Convergence is
1. The physical alignment of a number of planets with the sun, causing profound gravitational reactions, energy releases, and earth changes
2. An advanced position described in the Kama Sutra
3. A particularly difficult method of playing the harmonica
4. A fancy name for a barbershop quartet convention

It is speculated that the continent of Atlantis was destroyed and sank in the ocean due to
1. Its abuse of crystal energy and disruption of the balance of nature
2. The aloofness of its cultural elite
3. Shad-smoking among its teenagers
4. Gangsta rap

Which of the following characters does not appear in the Book of Revelation?
1. The Beast
2. The False Prophet
3. The Dragon
4. The Rifleman

As sightings of UFOs have increased in recent years, it has been speculated that aliens have been visiting us to help us usher in
1. A new era of global consciousness.
2. Discuss possible new sites for Wal-Mart
3. Protest their unfair depiction in Mars Attacks!
4. Tape Must See TV

Within the passageways of the Great Pyramid of Cheops, researchers have discovered
1. A physical chronology of the major events in world history
2. The Pharaoh's secret stash of adult hieroglyphics
3. Blood planted by the los Angeles Police Department
4. A new Starbucks
5.
According to surveys, most New Year's Eve 2015 were
1. Making elaborate resolutions
2. Being overserved
3. Shooting off handguns
4. Wondering how old Dick was when he died

SCORE
Score? Who cares about the score? Do you think this is from the Reader's Digest? Quit trying to show how smart you are. We're talking about the apocalypse here! If you want to impress people with your ready grasp of trivial knowledge, go on Jeopardy. If you want to know how and when the world is going to end, read my book, *Apocalypse Wow!* James Finn Garner

---

A Story from My Youth in Essex, North Carolina
(Population: 28)
Carol Leigh Alston Rados

When I was about four or five sometime in 1951 or 1952, I adopted and cared from any stray puppy that showed up in our yard. I fed them with milk from my doll bottle. One such adopted puppy was a rabbit dog. I was with my Dad at Mr. Luther Williams' store in Essex.

A neighbor came up and spoke to my Dad, Eugene Johnston Alston. "I notice that you have a rabbit dog. How much can I give you for him?"

Dad said, "Oh, that dog doesn't belong to me. He belongs to Carol Leigh," and pointed toward me.

The gentleman looked at me.

I said, "I'll let you have him if you'll give me a kitten."

The neighbor said, "I expect I can find a kitten somewhere around my place."

A few days later, the deal was done. He brought me a kitten and I gave him my rabbit dog.

My Dad never expressed any problem with my decision.

Crocus Dreams
Joan Leotta

If I had planted them
In fall
Instead of leaving them
In the garage
I would be marveling
At a panoply of gold
Purple, and white crocus
Flowers
Alas
My earlier indolence
Means the crocus will remain a dream
This spring
Next year, perhaps?

Why the Greeks?
Randy Bittle

The ancient Greeks were self-reliant people within a cultural framework that supported and reinforced individual achievement in cohesive community settings. Athenians thrived in this environment. They established the classical civilization between 500 B.C and 330 B.C. that became the foundation of modern Western Civilization. Writing ensured that the legacy endured for thousands of years, but you must keep in mind that the Greeks were, first and foremost, a speaking society. Spoken poetry, lyrics, speeches, and conversations enriched the lives of the people who forged the origins of Western tradition.

Every person who heard these vocal recitations interpreted them individually and discussed them with friends. It was a fertile environment for the growth of new ideas in the context of customary ritual and culture. Civic responsibility, inspired by the democratic form of government, promoted individual participation and self-reliance that led to a mature society of creative, interactive people. This differed from the formal, striated, and top-down controlled civilizations of Egypt and Mesopotamia.

Greek religion also differed from Egyptian and Mesopotamian theologies. The latter was closely run by castes of priests who allowed for little self-interpretation by common people. Greek theology, on the other hand, fostered understanding and implementation by ordinary citizens. The Oracle at Delphi exemplifies the personalized relationship between a citizen and the gods. Members of city-states all over Greece would travel to Delphi to get insight from the god Apollo on how to deal with problems in their daily lives. The priestess would chant out an answer unique to each question. To further emphasize active participation of citizens with the supernatural gods, the answer from the priestess had to be self-interpreted and appropriately applied to each situation.

Variations in lifestyles and administrations among the city-states added to the rich cultural heritage that gave birth to Western Tradition. Miletus was a colony city-state on the Western coast of Asia Minor (modern Turkey). Ideologies collided as the Greek culture was exposed to Middle East influences. Around 600 B.C., the first philosophers spoke and taught in the streets of Miletus. A theory is that the open exchange of ideas in the colony led to the birth of philosophy, but it wouldn't have happened without the initiatives of Thales and Anaximander, the first two known philosophers. Croton, another colony city-state located in Italy, was the home of the Pythagorean sect in the late sixth-century B.C.. Croton's government tolerated the Pythagorean cult that greatly influenced the intellectual development of Greece including Plato's ideas.

On the mainland, city-states also differed. Sparta's society was oriented around fighting wars. Their children were trained to fight before they were old enough to join the army. Sparta generated limited architecture, drama, poetry, written histories, artwork, and philosophy. On the other hand, Athens encouraged these activities and created lasting works that changed the world. Sophocles, Herodotus, Socrates, Plato, and Aristotle are all familiar names to educated people today, twenty-five centuries later.

In a collection of independent city-states with different lifestyles but a common heritage, tolerant of new ideas and pro-education, a few geniuses lived and wrote the classic poetry, drama, history, and philosophy that endures millennia afterwards. No single magic miracle occurred. It was the combination of factors unique to Ancient Greece that forged the birth of Western Tradition. Alexander the Great distributed that solid foundation to the world when he conquered it in the 330's B.C.

My Travel Plans for 2016
Unknown Source

1. I have been in many places, but I've never been in Kahoots. Apparently, you can't go alone. You have to be in Kahoots with someone.
2. I've also never been in Cognito. I hear no one recognizes you there.
3. I have, however, been in Sane. They don't have an airport; you have to be driven there. I have made several trips there, thanks to my children, friends, family, and work.
4. I would like to go to Conclusions, but you have to jump, and I'm not too much on physical activity anymore.
5. I have also been in Doubt. That is a sad place to go, and I try not to visit there too often.
6. I've been in Flexible, but only when it was very important to stand firm.
7. Sometimes I'm in Capable, and I go there more often as I'm getting older.
8. One of my favorite places to be is in Suspense! It really gets the adrenaline flowing and pumps up the old heart! At my age, I need all the stimuli I can get!

9. I may have been in Continent, but I don't remember what country I was in. It's an age thing. They tell me it is very wet and damp there. Probably smells bad, too.

Ann's Story
Diana Goldsmith

I was taking my dog for its last walk of the day. It was a quarter to four on Christmas Eve and the light was going. It was raining hard and there was a quite a strong wind. There was lots of mud on the ground and puddles of dirty water made it quite treacherous. Suddenly I was aware of the noise of a car approaching behind me. I managed to pull my dog over to the side of the road. When I looked, I could see that it was a police car.

"Excuse me," the officer asked. "But have you seen a woman about five foot three with a cast on her foot?"

"I'm sorry but I haven't as I have just walked through the estate and am only now starting my walk," I replied.

With a quick thank you, he closed the window and he drove off.

I continued on my way. I was deep in thought about this poor lady trying to walk along the lane when my concentration was broken by the sound of a helicopter overhead. It was circling high above the nature reserve. This is urgent as the police don't deploy the helicopter unless for a very good reason. Was she an old lady with dementia who had escaped from a nursing home or an escaped prisoner? Maybe she was even a terrorist! No, I had been watching too many TV crime programs.

I finished my walk and, as I didn't live far, I could still hear and see the police helicopter even to late in the evening. Fortunately, the weather was mild for late December. I mused to myself that I would probably hear something about it on the local news, but I didn't and the disappearing lady with the cast remained a mystery. It sounded like the title of a Sherlock Holmes novel.

New Year came and life went on and I had forgotten about this incident until I was enjoying a mug of hot chocolate with a friend I had bumped into in a local charity shop. We had decided to catch up by having a drink in a nearby café. We were talking about some of the people we encounter in our church's drop-in center where my friend is the receptionist and she started to tell me about Ann. Here is her story.

Ann Robinson was born in 1966 to a young girl called Lizzie who was only sixteen. Lizzie's mum was living on her own with six children and Lizzie was the oldest girl, she had two younger brothers and three sisters. Anyway, her mum expected her to help look after the children and she didn't want her to keep the baby as she was just another mouth to feed and, more importantly, in those days you couldn't be an unmarried mother, which would have meant her mum taking Ann on as her own. She had hoped that Lizzie would get a job down at the local factory, which would give extra income and help her fund her mother's alcohol addiction. So with Social Services intervention, Ann was fostered.

She was a plain baby with hair that stood on end and was loathe to be tamed. The babies that went for adoption, as there were very many then, were the pretty ones with angelic faces and curly hair and so she remained in foster care. For various reasons she had many foster placements and as she grew up it made her a resentful and difficult child, which increased the number of times she was removed from one family to another. As a teenager, she would often run away from her home and she trusted no one. She did however get to know other young people in similar situations and became very streetwise. She learned that drinking dulled the pain of loneliness and rejection. She even smoked cannabis, when she could get it, as she had been a smoker for many years. She funded these habits by stealing and later on by begging. She had left school or at least she had been expelled. She was sent to a hostel to live when she out grew the foster homes. However she hated it and left it and made her way to London. Here to fund her habits and to exist she found "friends" who introduced her to a life of prostitution. She hated the punters, especially those who abused her and she learned to take drugs to suppress the pain. She had many relationships with men she thought, misguidingly, that she could trust not to abuse her and some who even claimed to love her. However, these proved wrong assumptions. She became pregnant, but the first time her pimp made her have an abortion, as he wanted her working all the time. She was sent to a back street woman who used gin and knitting needles and she nearly died from a hemorrhage. The second time she kept her little girl and the father this time actually became fond of her in his way. He was a lot older than her, and had been one of her punters. He was an alcoholic too but agreed to look after her so she left the game and they managed to look after Stacey. It was hard going but somehow life took a turn for the better.

They managed to move from the London suburb where John had a council flat down to a country town in the West Country. John had managed to get an exchange and he also got a job in a local factory as did Ann. Stacey had left home having married and had gone to Australia to live. Then disaster. John suddenly dropped down dead from a heart attack at work. Ann took it very badly and all the past seemed to come back to haunt her. She turned to her old friend alcohol and became morose. She refused to go out or to eat properly or to care for herself. She used to wander the streets in an alcoholic stupor. She stank and often the police would find her when she had fallen over and was lying on the pavement or sometimes in the road. She was taken to the hospital to be patched up. She ended up one day breaking her leg when she fell down some steps. The hospital put a cast on it and she was able to walk on it by using a crutch. The trouble was that her mental state was so bad that she saw no future for herself. It was only the alcohol that blocked everything out. Now it was the worst time, Christmas Eve. She left her flat and walked with difficulty due to being three sheets to the wind and, also, trying to use a crutch on slippery muddy ground. She was heading for the reservoir when she slipped from the path and ended up in a stream. It was getting dark, and the effect of the cold water counteracted the effect of the alcohol and she felt the pain in her leg, which caused her to cry out. The policeman heard her as he was searching in the field by the reservoir and called an ambulance.

Ann ended up spending Christmas day in hospital and ironically really enjoyed it. Social Services got involved with her again and were really helpful and she was given food bags from the local churches to help her when she eventually went home to tide her over until Stacey could get over. She had decided to take her Mum back with her to start a new life in Australia. It was going to be a challenge for them both, but they were determined and not to let the past repeat itself.

""He who possesses virtue in abundance may be compared to an infant." Lao-tzu

From the Kitchen of P. L. Almanza
P. L. Almanza

Broccoli and Cheddar Chicken

Ingredients
4 boneless skinless chicken breasts
1 can of Campbell's Cheddar Cheese Soup
1 cup milk
1 1/2 cups Ritz Crackers
6 tablespoons of melted unsalted butter (you can use less)
8 ounces frozen broccoli
4 ounces shredded cheddar cheese

Instructions:
Preheat your oven to 350 degrees. Make can of Cheddar cheese soup mix according to package directions (one can of soup mix to one can of milk). Place chicken breasts in a baking dish. Pour 3/4 of the prepared soup over the chicken breasts. Add broccoli to chicken that has been covered with the cheddar soup. Melt butter and combine with Ritz crackers, sprinkle buttered crackers over the broccoli. Add remaining soup mix, and bake for approximately 45 minutes or until the chicken is done. When chicken has been removed from oven sprinkle with shredded cheddar cheese. Enjoy!

▲ ▶ ◀ ▼

Candy Brownies

INGREDIENTS:
1 Box fudge brownie mix and ingredients water, eggs and oil
½ stick butter, room temperature
2 cups confectioners' sugar
3 tbsp. milk - you can add a little more if needed for consistency
1 Bag Skittles

1 Bag Starburst Minis
1 Bag Snickers Minis- chopped
INSTRUCTIONS:
Preheat oven according to directions in your brownie recipe
Chop about 20 Snickers into quarters
Prepare brownies to package directions using a 10x10 square pan lined with parchment, leaving 1" overhang on the sides
After you add your brownie mix to the prepared pan, sprinkle on chopped Snickers and bake to recipe directions.
Remove brownies and allow to cool on wire rack in pan before adding frosting
While the brownies are cooling, prepare your frosting

Place softened butter in mixing bowl and beat until light and fluffy.
Add confectioners' sugar and mix until crumbly.
Add milk and beat on med-high until well incorporated and fluffy
Spread on cooled brownies
Sprinkle on your Skittles and Starburst candies
Remove brownies from the pan by lifting up on parchment
Cut into 16 even squares
Stack one on top of another to make a double decker!

Crock-Pot Pork Chops

Instructions:
Sprinkle dry Ranch Dressing over chops. Layer pork chops in a Crock-Pot. Add cream of chicken condensed soup. Cover and cook on high for 4 1/2 hours or on low for 6 1/2 hours.
The pork chops come out very tender and the flavor is amazing! You also get a good gravy for mashed potatoes or rice. Simple, delicious and worth the wait!
You can also cut up the chops and add mushrooms, olives, onions or any of your favorite things to eat with pork! Get creative! Bon Appetit!

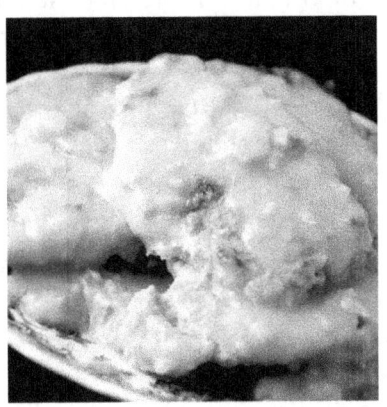

Lemon Zest Layer Cake

Ingredients
1¼ cups sifted all purpose flour
1½ cups sifted cake flour
½ teaspoon baking soda
1½ tsp baking powder
1½ cups sugar
⅔ cup vegetable oil
⅓ cup vegetable shortening at room temperature
1 tsp good quality vanilla extract
2 tsp pure lemon extract
3 large eggs
1½ cups buttermilk
zest one large lemon, grated and finely chopped
THE FROSTING
8 cups powdered sugar
2 cups unsalted butter
1 tsp pure lemon extract

1 tsp minced lemon zest
5 tbsp milk

Instructions

Grease and flour 2 nine inch round cake pans and line the bottom with 2 circles of parchment paper. Sift together both flours, baking soda. baking powder and sugar, Set aside.
In the bowl of an electric mixer beat together the vegetable oil, shortening, vanilla and lemon extract. Beat well at high speed with whisk attachment until light and fluffy
Beat the eggs in one at a time.
Fold in the lemon zest.
Fold in the dry ingredients alternately with the buttermilk.
Add the dry ingredients in three divisions and liquid ingredients in 2 divisions. It is very important to begin and end the additions with the dry ingredients. Do not over mix the batter.
When the batter is smooth, pour into the two prepared 9 inch cake pans.
Bake at 325 degrees for 35-45 minutes or until a wooden toothpick inserted in the center comes out clean. Allow the cake to cool in the pans for 10 minutes before turning out onto wire racks to cool completely.
Frosting instructions:
Mix together the icing sugar, lemon zest and butter until it becomes sort of crumbly.
Add the lemon extract and a little of the milk.
Beat until smooth and fluffy, adding only enough milk to bring the frosting to a creamy spreadable consistency.
Fill and frost the cake.
Garnish with candied lemon zest if desired.
To make candied lemon zest, remove the zest with a sharp vegetable peeler in long strips avoiding as much of the white pith as possible.
Bring one cup of water and one cup of sugar to a slow boil.
Add the pieces of lemon zest and boil for about 15 minutes. Drain the lemon zest on a wire rack. When cool, cut them in strips and roll in fine sugar.

Home Made Peach Dumplings

Ingredients:
2 whole large peaches
2 - 8 oz cans crescent rolls (you can use biscuits also)
2 sticks butter
1-1/2 cup sugar
1 tsp vanilla
Cinnamon (to taste)
1 - 12 oz can Mountain Dew

Peel and pit peaches. Cut peaches into 7 or 8 slices each. Roll each peach slice in a crescent roll. Place in a 9 x 13 buttered pan.

Melt the butter, then add sugar and vanilla, stir, then pour entire mixture over peaches. Pour Mountain Dew around the edges of the pan. Sprinkle with cinnamon and bake at 350 degrees for 45 minutes. Can serve with ice cream, and some of the sweet sauces from the pan over the top. Yummy!

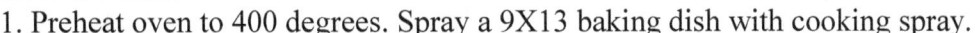

Loaded Chicken and Potatoes

Ingredients:
1 lb boneless chicken breasts - cubed
6-8 medium skin on red potatoes - cut in 1/2 cubes
1/3 cup olive oil
1 1/2 tsp salt *optional
1 tsp black pepper
1 Tbsp paprika
2 Tbsp garlic powder
3 Tbsp hot sauce
Topping:
2 cups fiesta blend cheese
1 cup crumbled bacon
1 cup diced green onion
How to Make:
1. Preheat oven to 400 degrees. Spray a 9X13 baking dish with cooking spray.
2. In a large bowl, mix together the olive oil, *salt, pepper, paprika, garlic powder, and hot sauce. Add the cubed potatoes and chicken and stir to coat. Carefully scoop the potatoes and chicken into the prepared baking dish..
3. Bake the potatoes and chicken for 55-60 minutes, stirring every 20 minutes, until cooked through, crispy, and browned on the outside. While the potatoes are cooking, fry your bacon (about half a pound).
4. Once the potatoes and chicken are fully cooked, remove from the oven. Top the cooked potatoes with the the cheese, bacon, and green onion. Return the casserole to the oven and bake for 5 minutes or until cheese is melted.
Serve With: extra hot sauce and/or ranch dressing or sour cream

Potato Soup

Ingredients
1 large onion diced
1 lb Italian sausage (mild or hot)
6 slices bacon diced
4 cups diced potatoes
3 cloves garlic
4 cups low sodium chicken broth
½ teaspoon crushed red peppers (optional)

1 cup heavy cream
2 cups torn & gently packed fresh spinach
pepper to taste

Instructions
In a large pot cook sausage and ½ of the onion until no pink remains. Drain and set aside.
Cook bacon over medium heat until most of the fat has been rendered out and drain. Add in potatoes, remaining onion, and garlic.
Stir in chicken broth, crushed peppers if using and sausage. Bring to a boil.
Reduce heat and simmer uncovered 12-14 minutes or until potatoes are softened.
Stir in heavy cream and let boil 1 minute. Remove from heat, stir in spinach.
Garnish with additional bacon if desired. Enjoy!

Simply Cheesecake

Ingredients:
Crust:
2 cups ground vanilla wafers or graham cracker crumbs
4 tablespoons unsalted butter, melted
1 pinch ground cinnamon (optional)
Filling:
2 (8 oz.) packages cream cheese, room temperature
1 (10 oz.) jar blueberry preserves (you can use strawberry or other preserves)
1 cup fresh blueberries (can use strawberry or other fresh fruits)
2/3 cup sugar
2 eggs
1 large lemon, zested and juiced
1 teaspoon vanilla extract (or whatever extract you like)

Directions:
Preheat oven to 350 degrees and grease a 9×13-inch baking dish with parchment paper, leaving a 2 1/2-inch overhang on both sides.
Place vanilla wafers in a large bowl and mix in melted butter and cinnamon until mixture is the consistency of damp sand.
Press mixture evenly into the bottom of greased baking dish to form the crust and refrigerate until later use.
In a large bowl or mixer (or using a food processor), beat cream cheese until smooth, then mix in eggs, sugar, lemon juice and zest until fully combined and incorporated.
Spread mixture over chilled crust and use an offset rubber spatula to even out the top.
Sprinkle fresh blueberries evenly over the cheesecake, then spread blueberry preserves on top.
Place baking dish in oven and bake for 30-35 minutes, or until the center is just set, but still jiggles.

Remove from oven and let cool completely before refrigerating at least 5 hours, or overnight. Use parchment paper overhang to extract cheesecake block from baking dish, cut into squares and serve chilled.

Spaghetti Muffins

For the Crust:
4 cups cooked spaghetti
1/3 cup melted butter
2 large eggs
1/2 cup parmesan cheese

Instructions:
Preheat oven to 350 degrees.
Mix together spaghetti and butter.
In a separate bowl, whisk eggs.
Add Parmesan cheese and mix well.
Pour egg mixture into spaghetti and butter mixture and mix well.
Spray 2 large muffin pans with cooking spray.
Divide spaghetti mixture evenly into 12 muffin cups.
Press spaghetti to form a little nest in each muffin cup.

The filling ingredients:
3/4 cup cottage cheese
1/4 cup parmesan cheese
Instructions:
Mix together both cheeses, spread over inside of spaghetti nests.
Sauce ingredients:
2 Tablespoons olive oil
1 pounds lean hamburger or sausage (I often use ground chicken or turkey)
1/2 tsp crushed dried basil
1/2 tsp garlic powder
1/2 tsp onion powder
1/2 tsp red pepper seeds
1/2 tsp salt, optional (I never add salt)
pepper to taste
1 15 oz can tomato sauce
1 cup Mozzarella Cheese

Instructions:
Pour olive oil into pan, add meat and seasonings and brown. Please use a very lean meat so that there is nothing to drain. But if you do have excess fat, go ahead and drain after it is browned.

Add tomato sauce.
Stir and simmer 10 minutes
Spoon evenly over spaghetti nests
Top each with mozzarella cheese.
Bake approximately 35 to 40 minutes until cheese is lightly browned. Let cool and serve warm. Enjoy!

Stuffed Strawberries

Ingredients:
1 8 oz. package cream cheese, softened
1/2 cup confectioners' sugar (powdered sugar)
1/2 teaspoon vanilla extract, or your favorite extract
1 pint fresh strawberries, hulled and cored
3 graham crackers, crushed, or your favorite topping
*Chocolate (optional but delicious).
Directions
Beat cream cheese, confectioners' sugar, and vanilla extract together in a bowl until smooth.
Spoon into a piping bag or a re-sealable bag with a corner snipped.
Fill cavities of cored strawberries with the cream cheese mixture. Sprinkle crushed graham crackers to coat.
Melt about 1/2 cup chocolate chips in a double boiler and drizzle over the strawberries.
*Optional

Trivia
Original Sources Unknown

1. Early aircraft throttles had a ball on the end of it, in order to go full throttle the pilot had to push the throttle all the way forward into the wall of the instrument panel. Hence "balls to the wall" for going very fast. And now you know the rest of the story.

2. During WWII, U.S. Airplanes were armed with belts of bullets which they would shoot during dogfights and on strafing runs. These belts were folded into the wing compartments that fed their machine guns. These belts measure 27 feet and contained hundreds of rounds of bullets. Often times, the pilots would return from their missions having expended all of their bullets on various targets. They would say, I gave them the whole nine yards, meaning they used up all of their ammunition.

3. Did you know the saying "God willing and the creek don't rise" was in reference to the Creek Indians and not a body of water? Benjamin Hawkins wrote it in the late 18th century. He was a politician and Indian diplomat. While in the south, Hawkins was requested by the President of the U.S. to return to Washington. In his response, he was said to write, "God willing and the Creek don't rise." Because he capitalized the word "Creek" he was referring to the Creek Indian tribe and not a body of water.

4. In George Washington's days, there were no cameras. One's image was either sculpted or painted. Some paintings of George Washington showed him standing behind a desk with one arm behind his back while others showed both legs and both arms. Prices charged by painters were not based on how many people were to be painted, but by how many limbs were to be painted. Arms and legs are 'limbs,' therefore painting them would cost the buyer more. Hence the expression, 'Okay, but it'll cost you an arm and a leg.' (Artists know hands and arms are more difficult to paint.)

5. As incredible as it sounds, men and women took baths only twice a year (May and October). Women kept their hair covered, while men shaved their heads (because of lice and bugs) and wore wigs. Wealthy men could afford good wigs made from wool. They couldn't wash the wigs, so to clean them they would carve out a loaf of bread, put the wig in the shell, and bake it for 30 minutes. The heat would make the wig big and fluffy, hence the term 'big wig'. Today we often use the term 'here comes the Big Wig' because someone appears to be or is powerful and wealthy.

6. In the late 1700's, many houses consisted of a large room with only one chair. Commonly, a long wide board folded down from the wall, and was used for dining. The 'head of the household' always sat in the chair while everyone else ate sitting on the floor. Occasionally a guest, who was usually a man, would be invited to sit in this chair during a meal. To sit in the chair meant you were important and in charge. They called the one sitting in the chair the 'chair man.' Today in business, we use the expression or title 'Chairman' or 'Chairman of the Board.'

7. Personal hygiene left much room for improvement. As a result, many women and men had developed acne scars by adulthood. The women would spread bee's wax over their facial skin to smooth out their complexions. When they were speaking to each other, if a woman began to stare at another woman's face she was told, 'mind your own bee's wax.' Should the woman smile, the wax would crack, hence the term 'crack a smile'. In

addition, when they sat too close to the fire, the wax would melt. Therefore, the expression 'losing face.'

8. Ladies wore corsets, which would lace up in the front. A proper and dignified woman, as in 'straight laced' wore a tightly tied lace.

9. Common entertainment included playing cards. However, there was a tax levied when purchasing playing cards but only applicable to the 'Ace of Spades.' To avoid paying the tax, people would purchase 51 cards instead. Yet, since most games require 52 cards, these people were thought to be stupid or dumb because they weren't 'playing with a full deck.'

10. Early politicians required feedback from the public to determine what the people considered important. Since there were no telephones, TV's or radios, the politicians sent their assistants to local taverns, pubs, and bars. They were told to 'go sip some Ale and listen to people's conversations and political concerns.' Many assistants were dispatched at different times. 'You go sip here' and 'You go sip there.' The two words 'go sip' were eventually combined when referring to the local opinion and, thus we have the term 'gossip.'

11. At local taverns, pubs, and bars, people drank from pint and quart-sized containers. A bar maid's job was to keep an eye on the customers and keep the drinks coming. She had to pay close attention and remember who was drinking in 'pints' and who was drinking in 'quarts,' hence the phrase 'minding your 'P's and Q's'.

12. One more: bet you didn't know this! In the heyday of sailing ships, all war ships and many freighters carried iron cannons. Those cannons fired round iron cannon balls. It was necessary to keep a good supply near the cannon. However, how to prevent them from rolling about the deck? The best storage method devised was a square-based pyramid with one ball on top, resting on four resting on nine, which rested on sixteen. Thus, a supply of 30 cannon balls could be stacked in a small area right next to the cannon. There was only one problem ... how to prevent the bottom layer from sliding or rolling from under the others. The solution was a metal plate called a 'Monkey' with 16 round indentations. However, if this plate were made of iron, the iron balls would quickly rust to it. The solution to the rusting problem was to make 'Brass Monkeys.' Few landlubbers realize that brass contracts much more and much faster than iron when chilled.. Consequently, when the temperature dropped too far, the brass indentations would shrink so much that the iron cannonballs would come right off the monkey; Thus, it was quite literally, 'Cold enough to freeze the balls off a brass monkey.'

13. Life is like a roll of toilet paper; the closer you get to the end the faster it goes.
Job Change: Last Wednesday a passenger in a taxi heading for Stafford station leaned over to ask the driver a question and gently tapped him on the shoulder to get his attention. The driver screamed, lost control of the cab, nearly hit a bus, drove up over the curb and stopped just inches from a large plate window. For a few minutes, everything was silent in the cab. Then the shaking driver said "Are you OK? I'm so sorry, but you scared the daylights out of me." The badly shaken passenger apologized to the driver and said, "I didn't realize that a mere tap on the shoulder would startle someone so badly." The driver replied, "No, no, I'm the one who is sorry, it's entirely my fault. Today is my very first day driving a cab. I've been driving a hearse for 25 years."

14. Old Geezer Opens Medical Practice: An old geezer became very bored in retirement and decided to open a medical clinic. He put a sign up outside that said: "Dr. Geezer's clinic. Get your treatment for $500, if not cured, get back $1,000."

Doctor "Young," who was positive that this old geezer didn't know beans about medicine, thought this would be a great opportunity to get $1,000. So he went to Dr. Geezer's clinic.

Dr. Young: "Dr. Geezer, I have lost all taste in my mouth. Can you please help me?"

Dr. Geezer: "Nurse, please bring medicine from box 22 and put 3 drops in Dr. Young's mouth."

Dr. Young: Aaagh!! -- "This is Gasoline!"

Dr. Geezer: "Congratulations! You've got your taste back. That will be $500."

Dr. Young is annoyed and goes back after a couple of days figuring to recover his money.

Dr. Young: "I have lost my memory, I cannot remember anything."

Dr. Geezer: "Nurse, please bring medicine from box 22 and put 3 drops in the patient's mouth."

Dr. Young: "Oh, no you don't, -- that is Gasoline!"

Dr. Geezer: "Congratulations! You've got your memory back. That will be $500."

Dr. Young (after having lost $1000) leaves angrily and comes back after several more days.

Dr.Young: "My eyesight has become weak --- I can hardly see anything!"

Dr. Geezer: "Well, I don't have any medicine for that so, "Here's your $1000 back." (giving him a $10 bill)

Dr. Young: "But this is only $10!"

Dr. Geezer: "Congratulations! You got your vision back! That will be $500."

The moral of this is it doesn't pay to try to outsmart old geezers.

Dove Hunting and Shotgunning
By Hurtford Smith Jr.
Reviewed by Tim Whealton

After I finished reading Dove Hunting and Shotgunning I feel like I'm able to put forth ideas on both shotgunning and dove hunting. I have been a gunsmith for over 45 years and I repair around one thousand guns each year. (No wonder I'm tired!) I am also a dove hunter. Not just an opening day dove hunter but a hunt till the last day dove hunter. I have hunted, killed, cleaned and cooked most everything that flies and is legal in North Carolina. There is nothing I enjoy more than a good dove hunt and my friends feel the same way.

Short version is I really like this book. While teaching gunsmithing at the college for several years I searched countless books about guns, shooting and hunting for students. Most were filled with lots of info you would never need and written by people that needed to ask others about what works and doesn't. Mr. Smith has done a great job of pruning away the useless information that can confuse you and tells you what works. His book looks small at first glance but it has every bit of the information you need to be a first class field shot on doves. If you can hit the gray-feathered rocket, you will be good to go on anything that flies.

Bottom line is you don't have to know everything that can go wrong. Just take the advice of a solid hunter and shooter. If you have one for a friend, you are blessed. If you don't, this book will tell you the same exact thing!

How do You Decide Who to Marry
Written by kids

You got to find somebody who likes the same stuff. Like, if you like sports, she should like it that you like sports, and she should keep the chips and dip coming. -- Alan, age 10

No person really decides before they grow up who they're going to marry. God decides it all way before, and you get to find out later who you're stuck with. -- Kristen, age 10

What is the right age to get married? Twenty-three is the best age because you know the person FOREVER by then. -- Camille, age 10

How can a stranger tell if two people are married? You might have to guess, based on whether they seem to be yelling at the same kids. -- Derrick, age 8

What do you think your mom and dad have in common? Both don't want any more kids. -- Lori, age 8

What do most people do on a date? Dates are for having fun, and people should use them to get to know each other. Even boys have something to say if you listen long enough. -- Lynnette, age 8 (isn't she a treasure)

On the first date, they just tell each other lies and that usually gets them interested enough to go for a second date. -- Martin, age 10

When is it okay to kiss someone? When they're rich. -- Pam, age 7 (Love her)

The law says you have to be eighteen, so I wouldn't want to mess with that. - Curt, age 7

The rule goes like this: If you kiss someone, then you should marry them and have kids with them. It's the right thing to do. - Howard, age 8

Is it better to be single or married?

It's better for girls to be single but not for boys. Boys need someone to clean up after them. -- Anita, age 9 (bless you, child)

How would the world be different if people didn't get married? There sure would be a lot of kids to explain, wouldn't there? -- Kelvin, age 8

And the #1 Favorite is ...

How would you make a marriage work? Tell your wife that she looks pretty, even if she looks like a dump truck. -- Ricky, age 10

Fire
Diana Goldsmith

Like flickering tongues it licks
savouring each mouthful with relish
then consuming hungrily it eats
until all is gone completely
leaving only ash.

Yellow, amber, orange and red
bright iridescent light
like the rainbow colours
contrasting strongly with the absolute
blackness of the night

Heat, red hot and branding
it burns skin to charred paper
flesh sears and blackens
and even the strongest steel
bends and melts at its command.

choking, acrid and breath taking
nostril flaring bitter tasting
eye watering vision blurring
unconsciousness occurring
death ensuing
job done fire has won!

C. S. Lewis

Christian theologian, C. S. Lewis had a down-to-earth sense of humor. His biographer, Walter Hooper, who grew up in Reidsville, NC, tells of the time Lewis gave a beggar some money. Hooper asked him if he was not concerned that the beggar would spend the money to buy whiskey. Lewis replied, "I don't know but if I kept the money that's what I would use it for."

Hammer Spade and the Long Shooter
E. B. Alston
Chapters Thirteen - Seventeen

The hotel lobby was nearly empty at five a.m. when Jack and Isabela checked out of the hotel. The night desk agent was nearing the end of his shift and barely noticed them while he was processing their paperwork. They talked about going to the airport to catch their plane. Isabela complained about the hour and why Jack was in such a hurry to leave a nice hotel.

Jack waved off the concierge saying they would prefer to carry their own luggage, a typical American trait of bargain travelers who didn't want to pay the tip. The concierge sneered when they walked past him out the door.

They walked to a Rover parked in a space reserved for check-in, loaded their luggage in the back and drove out of the hotel parking lot. They turned onto Highway 50 towards Bogotá. Nobody noticed that they didn't go toward the airport.

They had to be careful around Bogotá because there was a chance they might run into somebody who knew Isabela.

Isabela had set up a contact with a man in Florencia in the Department of Caquetá, which was southwest of Bogotá. Caquetá was a hotbed of intrigue associated with the cocaine business. FARC (Fuerzas Armadas Revolucionarias de Colombia) and AUC (Autodefensas Unidas de Colombia) were present in strength. Their presence made it very difficult to eradicate the cultivation of poppies.

They stopped for breakfast at a little restaurant in Los Amarillos.

"Isabela," Jack observed, "you are the most professional agent I have ever met."

"Thank you for the compliment," she replied with a smile. "Why do you say that?"

"Everything you have done has worked like clockwork. You got information about Lady Fisher's passage through Panama amazingly fast. You handled the robbery attempt better than the U.S. Special Forces. You got us out of Panama and into Colombia without leaving a paper trail. How long have you been in this business?"

She laughed. "This is my first case."

Jack was astonished. "First case!" he stammered. "What did you do before you took this assignment?"

"I'm a housewife. I worked for the embassy for a couple of years after I married but when my son Jason was born, I stopped working."

"How old is your son?"

"He's six."

"Who's looking after him while you're out in the boonies with me?"

"My husband and my mother."

Jack didn't say anything for a few seconds before he asked, "Where did you receive training for this?"

"Training?" she laughed. "I read every spy novel I could get my hands on."

"Did you read *Ashenden?*"

"As a matter of fact I did. It was most informative."

"Where did you learn to shoot?"

"My husband taught me."

"He must be a heck of a shot."

"He is a very good shot. He spent a whole day teaching me how to shoot."

"One whole day," Jack mused. "I know people who have practiced for years who can't shoot as well as you can."

"My husband said I was a natural."

"I'm sure he was right. You chewed me out for being unprofessional that morning when I wandered around in La Palma looking like a gringo tourist."

"Yes, I did, and I was right. If you had been arrested or kidnapped, it would have wrecked this whole project and ruined any chance for us to find Lady Fisher."

Jack grinned. "You are some woman, Isabela."

She returned his smile. "And you are some man, Mr. Kane." She paused. "It was fun being Mrs. Kane last night."

"Yeah, it was a very pleasant evening, Isabela," Jack agreed.

Jack called for the check, tipped the waiter and paid at the cash register. Then they drove west towards Florencia.

▼▲▼▲▼

Chapter Fourteen

They arrived in Florencia at noon and checked with the local British consulate for messages. Finding none, they drove to a farm a few miles outside the city owned by Carlos Abadia, one of Isabela's distant relatives. Carlos was a rotund man who obviously ate well. He greeted Isabela as if she were his favorite rich relative.

"And how is your mother?" he inquired.

"Mother is fine and she sends you her love."

"Your mother has done well for herself," Carlos said. "Who is your friend?"

"This is Jack Kane. He is an American who is looking for a farm in Colombia."

"A farm? Why yes, there are several farms available in this area. They are in possession of banks because the United States drove their owners into bankruptcy. The Americanos and our government destroyed their cash crop."

"You mean the poppy crop?" Jack asked.

"Yes. The fruit of the poppy is more lucrative than coffee."

"Do you have time to show Mr. Kane around?" Isabela asked.

"I would be pleased to do anything you ask, Isabela," Carlos replied.

Jack got into the back seat and Carlos got in the front seat to give Isabela directions.

After they were underway, Carlos asked Jack, "What will you plant on a farm in Colombia?"

"Poppies."

"You, an American, plan to grow poppies in Colombia?"

"Sure."

"What about your government interdiction programs? How will you prevent the destruction of your crops?"

"I have inside connections."

"Oh, ho!" Carlos exclaimed. "You are a man after my own heart. An Americano with connections." He turned and faced Jack. "We must become acquainted, Mr. Kane. I have many friends who would like to know an American with 'connections'. They would pay you handsomely if you used your connections on their behalf."

"I have to find a farm first."

"I will assist you. It is a pleasure meeting you."

"I'm also looking for a contact in the 'business.' Do you know a man named Jaime Orjuela?"

Carlos frowned. "Unfortunately, you are too late to meet with Señor Orjuela."

"Too late?"

"Yes. Señor Orjuela was involved in a tragic accident a week and a half ago."

"Accident?"

"Yes, his pickup was found submerged in the river and Señor Orjuela was inside."

"Dead?"

"Yes. Three days in the river will kill a man."

"That's tough luck for me."

"Why is it tough luck for you, Señor Kane?"

"Now I've got to find somebody else."

"I am afraid I do not know anybody else with Señor Orjuela's talents, Señor Kane."

"Then I guess we'll have to go to Caqueza next, won't we, Isabela?"

"Yes. But we still need to look for a farm."

"Then I can help you with that," Carlos replied.

It was lunch-time and they went to a local restaurant where Carlos ordered two of everything.

After lunch they toured the countryside looking at farms until four p.m. When they were leaving, Isabela slipped a hundred dollars to Carlos, thanked him for his hospitality and said goodbye. They booked rooms in a small hotel in Florencia. It had a restaurant where they ate the local specialty, drank the local wine and went to bed at nine-thirty.

The next morning they were up at seven having breakfast in the restaurant.

"How do you feel this morning?" Jack asked.

"I feel great. How about you?"

"I'm okay too. I dread the long drive. How far is it to Caqueza?"

"Around two hundred miles. We'll make good time after we get to Highway 40."

"Who are we going to meet?"

"Another cousin of mine."

"You must have been assigned to this because of your family and tribal connections."

"Members of my mother's family and their tribe are all over Colombia."

"I wouldn't have accomplished anything without you on this trip. If you quit, I might as well go home."

"Thank you. It has been fun so far."

"Even the gunfight in the jungle?"

"I wasn't afraid. Maybe my husband was right. I am a natural."

"If they had captured you, you might not feel that way. A pretty woman would be a big catch for men like them."

"If my family got word that I was captured, they would rescue me."

Jack laughed. "You are a piece of work, Isabela."

"Exactly what is a 'piece of work'?"

"You are a very unique individual."

"So are you," she laughed. She looked at her watch. "We had better get moving."

Jack called for the check.

▲▼▲▼▲

Chapter Fifteen

The first part of their drive was arduous along mud and dirt roads. Jack and Isabela didn't talk much because she was concentrating on driving as he watched the spectacular scenery. Isabela relaxed after they got to Highway 40. It was a major route and there was a steady flow of traffic on the highway.

"Back to civilization," Isabela remarked.

"Which one are we hunting in Caqueza?"

"Juan Garcia."

"Who's your local relative?"

"Pilar Santos. He is my first cousin."

"Is he a farmer?"

"No."

"What does he do for a living?"

"He works for the Cartel."

Jack was about to say this was a bad choice but realized that this man knew more about what was going on than anybody else.

"He probably knows more than your typical farmer."

"It's his job to know who comes and goes in his district."

"Does he already know about me?"

"He knows of you, but not your mission."

"Did you tell him about me?"

"He already knew you were in Colombia."

"Isabela, you continue to amaze me."

"Why? I'm just doing my job."

"Your husband was right. You are a natural."

She smiled, "Thank you."

"But you still don't strike me as the type for this kind of work."

"You barely know me. Why do you say I'm not the type?"

"Because you are the most wholesome woman I know."

"Wholesome? Does that matter? Why would it matter?"

"Not as far as I'm concerned. Your wholesomeness is very appealing. It would put people off their guard."

"I was brought up to be wholesome. My behavior the last few days is not normal behavior for me."

"Is that so?"

"Yes. My mother grew up in a village where all the houses had dirt floors. My father rescued her and made her an Englishwoman. To my knowledge they have never looked at anybody else. I admire my mother because she managed to acclimate to the English culture very successfully."

"That is admirable," Jack agreed.

"I admire my father because he recognized my mother's talents and was proud of her. He never disparaged her because of her humble origin.

"I have tried to make my life a model of theirs. My husband is a good man. To my knowledge, he has never looked at anybody else. He is at home now caring for our son. When this case is over and I return home, he will be happy."

She paused to give Jack a chance to comment, but he didn't.

"I have known you for less than a week. You have put ideas into my head that I must resist. I thank you for respecting my wishes that first night in La Palma. If you had touched the hem of my skirt, I would have been yours that night. But you were a gentleman. I lay awake half the night trying to convince myself not to go to you while I was wishing that you would come to me."

"I thought about you too, Isabela, but we're working on a dangerous project in a dangerous place. And…," he stopped talking.

"And what?"

"We ought to end this kind of talk, Isabela."

"Why?" She insisted that he explain.

"You are the nicest woman I have ever met, Isabela. It would be wrong of me to ruin your life."

She started to say, "Suppose I agreed?" but she knew that Jack was right and instead replied, "Thank you for thinking of my welfare and my family's."

"You appeal to me, too, Isabela, but I am an honest man who considers you a friend and I will never cause trouble for a friend."

"Your friendship is precious to me, Jack."

"And yours to me, Isabela. And we must change the subject."

They were getting close to Caqueza and traffic was heavy. They were to meet Pilar for dinner. Jack hoped they would get some useful information about the whereabouts of Lady Margot Fisher.

▼▲▼▲▼

Chapter Sixteen

They drove into Caqueza in late afternoon. It was a town of about five thousand, nestled in a lush valley between two mountains south of Highway 40 where it meets the road to Ubaque. Tourist wise, it was similar to La Palma with no modern hotels. The town had bright-colored, excellently maintained municipal buildings.

They stopped at a market where Isabela asked directions to a local inn. After they were settled in their rooms, Isabela called her cousin and got directions to a restaurant where they could eat and talk.

When they arrived at the restaurant, they were met by a smiling man about Jack's age. He gave Isabela an enthusiastic family hug, then he stood back and looked at her.

"Isabela, you grow more beautiful with each passing day."

"And you more handsome, Pilar."

"And how are your mother and grandparents?"

"Mother is at home caring for my son, Jason, while I'm on this assignment," Isabela said. "My grandfather and grandmother are at home as usual."

"How old are they?"

"In their seventies. Grandfather still grows a big vegetable garden and keeps a horse."

"A horse? At his age? He is still the *caballero andante*."

Isabela laughed. "He rides his horse to the market every day."

"Your grandfather gave me my first ride on a horse. I was ten and afraid of horses. He whispered in my ear that the horse was afraid of me and I must not let him know of my fear."

"How is your family?"

"We are the same. Uncle Pablo is dead." Pilar looked at Jack. "The Americano butchers killed him."

"I am very sorry to hear that Pablo is dead." She paused, "This is Jack Kane. He is an American and we are working together."

Pilar shook Jack's hand. "Because you are with Isabela, I will shake your hand in friendship but I do not like the Americanos." Then he smiled at Isabela, "I have a table where we can eat and talk in private."

They followed Pilar to a small private dining room like you'd expect a Colombian Al Capone to use. After they took their seats, a waiter served the wine and took their orders.

"Tell me of your fine son," Pilar asked.

"He is six. He does well in his studies and is in an advanced class. He looks like my husband but he acts like my grandfather."

Isabela produced a photograph of a robust looking boy with a light complexion and hair as black as soot.

"He has your beautiful hair," Pilar exclaimed. "Such a handsome son. You must be proud."

A beaming Isabela agreed, "I am a proud mother."

"Will there be more fine children to follow this one?" Pilar asked.

"Yes. My husband wants four. I want two."

"Such a lovely mother as yourself must make many handsome sons and beautiful daughters for posterity."

Isabela laughed. "Not this mother."

Pilar turned to Jack. "Do you have sons and daughters, Señor Kane?"

"No, just me. I don't stay in one place long enough to have a family."

Pilar gave Jack a knowing smile. "Señor Kane, I know what kind of man you are. You are a man of the world and somewhere there are lively, intractable, unruly children who call other men their father."

"I wouldn't know about that."

Their meals came and Isabela and Pilar continued their family discussion while Jack ate and listened.

After they finished dinner, the waiter brought another bottle of wine, opened it, and then left, closing the door.

"Isabela tells me that you are looking for Lady Margot Fisher," Pilar said, getting down to business.

"That's right."

"Lady Margot Fisher has visited our area and we believe she has left."

"How do you know that?"

"Because Juan Garcia was murdered nine days ago. A man who worked for him was murdered also and we believe Lady Fisher was responsible."

"We always seem to be two weeks behind her," Jack said.

"And we too, seem to follow her cold trail, Señor Kane. We also seek Lady Fisher. Lady Fisher is a vicious, cruel, cold-blooded murderer."

"She is punishing men who arranged the murder of her family," Jack replied.

"But she was the first to murder. She murdered Señor Kurt Dietrich in the presence of the woman he loved. And she did it from nine soccer fields away. That was cold-blooded murder, Señor Kane. Señor Dietrich had done no harm to Lady Fisher or her family."

"I cannot discuss the merits or the morality of what has happened," Jack replied. "I cannot change anything either. All that is in the past and the past is fixed. My job is to find Lady Fisher and take her home."

"We too are seeking Lady Fisher. If we find her first, Lady Fisher will not go home." Pilar paused. "I respect you, Señor Kane, because you speak with candor and because my beloved cousin Isabela respects you, but we have different missions. I believe fate will determine who finds Lady Fisher first." He then stood up and downed his glass of wine.

"Señor Kane, I truly hope that you and I do not locate Lady Fisher at the same time."

Then Pilar left the room and closed the door behind him.

▲▼▲▼▲

Chapter Seventeen

There was no direct route to Curillo. Jack and Isabela drove northeast toward Florencia, then wandered north on mountain roads to Route 65 where they turned southwest.

Driving conditions were better on Route 65 and they could talk.

"Isabela, are you Catholic?" Jack asked.

"Yes," she replied.

"I've never asked this of a Catholic before. Why are you a Catholic and not a Presbyterian or Baptist or Methodist?"

"I was brought up Catholic and I respect the Church's unbroken connection all the way back to Saint Peter, who the Savior chose as his successor. I agree with the Church's teaching that both God and man have free will. I also agree that both revealed scripture and tradition are important beliefs."

"What about the Church abuses during the second millennium?"

"The Church is a human organization and it can commit error."

"Isn't that dangerous?"

"Certainly, but scripture and tradition endured during the trouble. God-fearing souls were saved, as they always are."

"You have a logical mind, Isabela. I admire that."

"Thank you."

He laughed. "And I agree with your cousin, Pilar, that you are beautiful."

"Thank you, again."

"Are we meeting another cousin tomorrow?"

"No. We're meeting a contact that Clover gave me. I don't know him."

"What's his name?"

"Jorge Carver."

"That's not an Indian or Spanish surname."

"That doesn't mean anything here. He could be the descendant of a shipwrecked English sailor from five hundred years ago and an Indian or Spanish woman."

"I guess he could at that. Is this meeting in the boonies or in town?"

"It's in a tiny village about two hours from Curillo."

"Two hours on a road like this or two hours on roads like those around La Palma?"

She laughed. "It's less than twenty miles."

"You sure can drive on these mountain roads. How did you learn to drive on dirt roads so well?"

"I learned to drive during the winters when my mother stayed with my grandparents. All the roads where my grandparents live are like those around La Palma."

"I hope we get a real lead on the whereabouts of Lady Fisher this time. I feel like we've been chasing a phantom."

"She has been very elusive."

"You can say that again."

They followed Highway 65 until they came to the Marquetalia exit. They continued southwest on treacherous roads through El Dorado, Bellavista and Santa Marta. They had lunch in El Dorado and dinner in Santa Marta. They finally arrived after dark in Curillo, a small town on Rio Caqueta.

It was almost eleven p.m. by the time they got a room in a local hotel. They had to share a room with one bed because the hotel had only one vacancy. Jack sat outside on the veranda while Isabela took her bath and got into bed. Then he came inside and took his bath. He slept on a pallet on the floor. It was after midnight by the time he got to sleep.

They were up and on the road at dawn. The road was a rough, rutted track that had to be driven in four-wheel drive most of the time.

An hour from Curillo, they came upon a car with its hood up, partially blocking the trail. A woman was standing in front of the car looking at something under the hood.

"She must be in trouble," Jack said. "Maybe I can give her a hand."

Isabela stopped slightly behind the stranded vehicle and both of them got out of the Rover.

Isabela asked the woman what was wrong. The woman replied that she didn't know. When Jack moved to the front of the vehicle, the woman moved back to allow him to look under the hood. When Jack leaned over to look at the engine, the woman kicked him twice in the calf of his leg, and then she ran.

"What did she do, Jack?" Isabela asked.

"She pricked my leg with something," Jack replied.

Isabela drew her pistol and shot the fleeing woman in the back. When the woman tried to get up, Isabela shot her three more times.

"Why did you do that?" Jack asked.

"She stuck you with a poison dart. Find something you can use for a tourniquet and get in the Rover. I have got to take you to a hospital."

While Jack rummaged for a tourniquet, Isabela ran to the dead woman and removed the woman's right shoe. Then she ran back to the Rover and showed the shoe to Jack. The shoe had a sharpened roofing nail sticking through the toe.

"Put the tourniquet on just below your knee. Loosen it every fifteen minutes for five minutes. I can't help you with it. I have got to drive."

Isabela got on her cell phone and dialed a number.

When the duty officer answered, she said, "This is 5030. I believe 0063 has been wounded by a poisoned nail. I am taking him to the hospital in Curillo. I am about an hour away."

Isabela paused and listened.

"I have the shoe with the nail in it."

They said something else.

"She is dead," Isabela replied.

She listened.

"I killed her. She is lying in the road in front of a Toyota automobile with its hood up."

She listened again.

"We didn't see anybody else."

She listened.

"It was a setup."

They asked another question.

"Pilar Diego."

Isabela listened again. She then hung up the phone, got into the Rover, turned around, and drove down the rough road. God help anybody who got in Isabela's way that day.

"How do you feel?" she asked Jack.

"My leg is getting numb."

"How's your breathing?"

"Okay."

"How's your vision."

"The light hurts my eyes."

As they entered Curillo, she asked Jack a question and he didn't respond. When she drove up to the emergency entrance of the hospital, two attendants and a doctor were waiting. They quickly removed Jack from the Rover, strapped him onto the gurney and wheeled him into the hospital.

Another doctor asked her for the shoe and told her that a helicopter from the British Embassy was on the way with a doctor who was familiar with poisons.

Isabela parked the Rover and went inside the waiting room where she began a long wait. She heard a helicopter land. Medics and another doctor rushed in. Five minutes later, they came out with Jack and five minutes after that, she heard the helicopter leave.

In their urgent haste, nobody noticed Isabela or thought to tell her what was going on. A few minutes after the helicopter left, Isabela got up and went to the Rover. She remembered passing an old, red brick church with two bell towers on the edge of town. She drove to the church, went inside, kneeled at the altar and prayed.

A priest came to her.

"Señora, are you troubled?"

"Yes, I am, Father."

"What troubles you?"

"A man I love may die."

"Is this man your husband?"

"No. I have not loved this man as I love my husband."

"Is he a good man, Señora?"

"Yes, he is a good man."

"Is he protected by the arms of the Church?"

"No, Father, he is not."

"Does he love the Lord?"

"He honors God with his honest heart."

"If he is a good man in his heart, Señora, he will rest in the arms of our Savior."

"He is a good man in his heart, Father."

"Señora, your faith and his pure heart will protect him from all evil."

"Thank you, Father."

"I will say a Mass for him this evening. What is this man's name?"

"Jack Kane."

Continued next Issue – Part Three – Dave Quigley

Starting Over
Tim Whealton

You wonder sometimes if you can just start your life over. What would you do differently? Is it too late? Can I do it? What will my friends think? Am I too old? Will it be any better? Will I screw it up worse and a million other questions that pop up. You start to dream about how you could fix every problem now that you know all about life. You can simply avoid the problems before they even happen.

Probably if you are old enough to read this, you know problems and life go hand in hand. If you think starting over will let you avoid the problems you had better stay where you are. You will take your problems with you and add more. I know, I have done it several times! Some because I wanted too, some because I had no choice. I'm not qualified to give advice because all I learned is that I don't know the best way to start over. Luckily I never let not knowing how stop me from doing anything.

The best example of starting over in my family has to be my daughter Susan. She did it with a family of 4 and has made it work. She was working in real estate at Ocracoke, NC. Her husband James was born on Ocracoke and never lived anywhere else. With a 13-year-old son and a 7 year old daughter I was sure they would stay on Ocracoke till retirement. With a lot of planning and a lot of guts they left everything they knew and moved the family to Alaska. I can't imagine a more drastic move without leaving the USA.

But why would anyone want to leave a paradise destination like Ocracoke? It has spectacular beaches, saltwater fishing, lots of visitors' spending money and beauty. While it is wonderful to visit it is hard to stay. Everything has to come and go on the ferry. Being a playground for the rich has made the property values climb above anything working people can afford. If you want anything more than lunch or ice and beer, you have to go get it. That takes a day! With only 6-10 children in each grade, there just aren't many things for kids to do on their own.

After they made one visit to Alaska, they were committed to changing their lives for the future of their children. They left everything they knew and moved. Taking only a few possessions they sold everything else and bought one way tickets and rode the ferry for the last time. They didn't have jobs, family for support, vehicles or a home. They did have confidence in their abilities and it was that confidence that made it possible.

When they left they took two friends with them. Both were volunteers that had special skills. When they landed they started the task of finding vehicles and setting up a home in a rental house. Then the volunteers went home and they started the more daunting task of finding a home and jobs. They were uniquely qualified for these task. Susan has worked on computer networks, waitress jobs, real estate agent, rental agent, store owner, and book keeper and Mom. James has more abilities than I can describe but his most impressive is he can design and build anything from a 3-story house to a go cart and likes to work at a pace that scares most people. Ocracoke people seem to shift gears as the seasons change and that mentality probably helped.

Since it was August when they left I was concerned about them going through their first long dark Alaskan winter. When the sun comes up at 10am and sets at 3pm and only climbs slightly above the trees, it has to be a different world. But this crew seems to thrive on change and adaptation. The pictures tell the story. Arabella has learned ice skating, Jamie has become a basketball star, Susan was hired by a 24x7 veterinary hospital and then moved to another job with the gas company. Her old job tried to hire her back and the new job gave her a raise before her first day. James used his skills to repair the home they bought at a bargain and now has gone to work with a construction company. The pictures show that a family who use to try to get stuff has changed and now they are trying to do stuff. It has changed everything and they are all thriving!

Now the question is did Alaska bring the change or did the change bring Alaska? I know from talking with many people that have made major changes in life that it always starts with a phrase that is present in every story. It's only two words but they are important and powerful. The words are "I decided." It's that point where you stop dreaming and put your plan into action. That point takes the most courage. You risk losing if you try to change. But if you don't make a change, you risk keeping a life you're not happy with. That might be the biggest disaster of all!

Why Can't Women be Assertive and Men be Feisty

Leigh Jean Russell
Women and men face double standards.

Men who put themselves forward at work are "assertive." Women who do the same are more often "pushy" or "bossy." Men are "persistent." Women "nag." Men are "frustrated," women "upset." A man has a lot to say. A woman is "chatty." A man discusses the doings of his colleagues and rivals. Women "gossip."

If you might be tempted to doubt this, you can check for yourself. If you want to check this out, you can do your own survey. Type "gossip" into Google, click on "images" and see who appears to be doing it. Try the same with "nagging" and "bossy." For hard data, try Google's "ingram" viewer, which shows the frequency of words and phrases among the hundreds of billions of words in the books scanned by Google, spanning centuries. One of the most common words following "gossiping" is "old." And the most common words to follow "gossiping old" are, in this order: "women," "woman," "men," "lady," and "ladies."

Some words are trickier than mere double standards. Those using them may think they are paying a kind of compliment, whereas what is heard is something between condescension and insult A case in point is "feisty." Those who use it might think that the word connotes "spirited." It is often heard by women, though, as carrying a whiff of surprise that a woman would show such spirit.

"Nonsense," some will reply. Recently *The Economist* used "feisty" to refer to Greece's leftist government, a South African tabloid, a (male) Argentinian presidential candidate, and Singaporean opposition bloggers. But it is also used fairly frequently with female figures. The common thread seems to be a sense of smallness or underdog status. When was the last time you read that a jowly dictator or heavyweight boxer was "feisty"? Google's book data say much the same. "Little" is one of the most common words to follow "feisty," and the most common words to follow "feisty little" are "girl," "man," "thing," "guy," "woman," and "lady." Rounding out the top ten words following "feisty little" are "Irishman" and "bastard." This says plainly if you should call anyone "feisty," and especially a woman. If you want to pay a female a sincere compliment, feisty is not the word. If you really want to get through to a man, call him feisty because the word's feminine associations are especially condescending. Feisty belittles and feminizes the same time. For an unmixed compliment, try "passionate" or "outspoken."

Other words can carry a compliment and an unwelcome sideswipe at the same time. Those who are "spry" are not just lively, but "lively for their advanced age." Those who are "jolly" or "jovial" are more often pot-bellied than stick-thin. "Statuesque" women may or may not appreciate the reminder that they are tall or full-figured. "Bubbly" and "vivacious" go beyond cheerful to imply a lack of seriousness. And if there is a compliment that black Americans resent above all, it is "articulate," which is heard carrying a note of surprise.

A widespread habit of lightly taking offence can be a burden on everyone. Take the debate over "micro aggressions" on American university campuses, defined as the small humiliations minority students endure. These might be described as too small for the speaker to notice, yet too big for the hearer to ignore. On one hand, some insults are clearly real – a student from California being asked where she is "really" from, because of an Asian-American face.

On the other side of this subject, two sociologists, Bradley Campbell and Jason Manning, produces a paper in 2014 that a "culture of victimhood" is replacing the "culture of dignity."

Harvard is currently seeking to rename the faculty members who oversee student halls because their traditional title, "house masters," re-minds some of slavery. Steven Pinker, a psychologist and language scholar at Harvard, tweeted drily that "1) All words have more than one meaning. 2) Mature adults must resist taking pointless offence."

It is a waste of time to score this debate entirely in favor of the micro aggressors or their victims. The bottom line is, it always pays to choose words well. Calling an opinionated woman "feisty" need not be micro-aggression. In all probability, it is often just lazy. Thoughtfully searching for the right word, free of off-notes, does much more than avoid offence. It makes speakers and writers scour their minds for original and arresting language. This is a good thing in itself.

Student Who Got Zero
Unknown Source

I would have given him 100%! Each answer is absolutely grammatically correct and funny too. The teacher had no sense of humor.

Q1: In which battle did Napoleon die? * His last battle

Q2: Where was the Declaration of Independence signed? * at the bottom of the page

Q3: River Ravi flows in which state? * Liquid

Q4: What is the main reason for divorce? * Marriage

Q5: What is the main reason for failure? * Exams

Q6: What can you never eat for breakfast? * Lunch & dinner

Q7: What looks like half an apple? * The other half

Q8: If you throw a red stone into the blue sea, what will it become? * Wet

Q9: How can a man go eight days without sleeping? * No problem, he sleeps at night.

Q10: How can you lift an elephant with one hand? * You will never find an elephant that has one hand.

Q11: If you had three apples and four oranges in one hand and four apples and three oranges in other hand, what would you have? * Very large hands

Q12: If it took eight men ten hours to build a wall, how long would it take four men to build it? * No time at all, the wall is already built.

Q13: How can you drop a raw egg onto a concrete floor without cracking it? * Any way you want, concrete floors are very hard to crack.

On the other hand, I have never met, or heard, of a teacher who liked smart alecks.

The Bulwer-Lytton Fiction Contest
Where "WWW" means "Wretched Writers Welcome"

Conceived to honor the memory of Victorian novelist Edward George Earl Bulwer-Lytton and to encourage unpublished authors who do not have the time to write books, the contest challenges entrants to compose bad opening sentences to imaginary novels. Bulwer was selected as patron of the competition because he opened his novel "Paul Clifford" (1830) with the immortal words, "It was a dark and stormy night." Lytton's sentence actually parodied the line and went on to make a real sentence of it, but he originated the line "The pen is mightier than the sword," and the expression "the great unwashed." His best known work is "The Last Days of Pompeii" (1834), an historical novel that has been adapted for film multiple times.

As has happened every year since the contest went public in 1983, thousands of entries poured in not just from the United States and Canada but from such countries as England, Australia, New Zealand, Switzerland, Germany, Japan, Ireland, and Indonesia.

2015 Contest Winners

Winner:

Seeing how the victim's body, or what remained of it, was wedged between the grill of the Peterbilt 389 and the bumper of the 2008 Cadillac Escalade EXT, officer "Dirk" Dirksen wondered why reporters always used the phrase "sandwiched" to describe such a scene since there was nothing appetizing about it, but still, he thought, they might have a point because some of this would probably end up on the front of his shirt. — Joel Phillips, West Trenton, NJ

The winner of the 33rd edition of the Bulwer-Lytton Fiction Contest is Joel Phillips of West Trenton, New Jersey. An Alabama native, Joel teaches music theory.

Runner-Up:

We can't let the dastards win," said Piper Bogdonovich to her fellow gardener, Mr. Sidney Beckworth Hammerstein, as she clenched her gloved hands into gnarly, fuzzed fists, "because if I have to endure another year after which my Royal Puffin buttercups come in second place to Marsha Engelstrom's Fainting Dove Tear Drop peonies, I will find a machine gun and leave my humanity card in the Volvo." — Grey Harlowe, Salem, OR

Grand Panjandrum's Special Award:

Ozymandias looked upon his mighty statue and despaired, amazed that the sculptors could have gotten his nose so wrong and wishing the darned thing would just crumble into pieces and blow across the lone and level sands, but leaving his legs since they were actually rather flattering. — Margaret Stein, Omaha, NE

Winner, Adventure:

After weeks at sea, Captain Fetherstonhaugh and his hardy crew had at last crossed the halfway point, and he mused that the closest dry land now lay in the Americas, assuming of course that it was not raining there. — David Laatsch, Baton Rouge, LA

Runner-Up, Adventure:

Certainly most people in Morris' place would have had certain misgivings about being stranded aboard a life raft, facing the unrelenting hunger and the possibility of having to eat the weaker members of the crew just to eke out the chance of survival for a few more days, but as Morris was an Asiatic black bear he had absolutely no qualms about it whatsoever. — Charlie Hill, Auckland, New Zealand

Dishonorable Mentions, Adventure:
A thousand miles from the coast a cheer went up from the burned, ragged survivors of the Cortez party as they descended upon the hapless prairie dog devouring skin, fur, blood, everything in their ravenous quest for sustenance since their expulsion, two months previously, from the Reno Holiday Inn without the concomitant expulsion from the safe of their wallets and passports.— Dave Hurt, Leicester, UK

If old Elijah's warning about the North Korean cruise ship of Liberian registry, crewed by Thai slaves wasn't enough, dinner at the Somali Captain's table in a lifeboat near confirmed it.— Paul Ross, Santa Fe, NM

Walking through the northernmost souk of Marrakech, that storied and cosmopolitan city so beloved of voyagers wishing to shake the desert dust off their feet, Peter bought a French-language newspaper and realized, with dizzying dismay, that "Camille" can be a man's name. — Myriam Nys, Mechelen, Belgium

Winner, Children's Literature:
The doctors all agreed the inside of Charlie's intestinal tract looked like some dark, dank subway system in a decaying inner city, blackened polyps hanging from every corner like tiny ticking terrorist time bombs, waiting to burst forth in cancerous activity; however, to Timmy the Tapeworm this was home. — E. David Moulton, Summerville, SC

Runner-Up, Children's Literature:
Shortly after that interfering do-gooder Snow White had introduced Sneezy to non-drowsy antihistamines, he had to change his name to Brian, where he then left the mines with Ray (formerly Sleepy) who was now a caffeine addict and Bob (formerly Grumpy) who was on 100 milligrams of Prozac a day, and Doc whom Snow pointed out had never actually graduated from medical school and was being sued for malpractice--oh how he despised that high and mighty ho. — Hwei Oh, Sydney, Australia

Dishonorable Mentions, Children's Literature:
The three little pandas followed Nanny Wei Wong down the grassy path towards the lotus pool, bathing suits, rubber duckies, and favorite bamboo sandwiches safely in their panda packs -- how they loved their school break -- but they had no idea what was waiting for them this summer, just over the Big Bear Bridge!— Linda Gorman, Albuquerque, NM

As Granny sewed the bloody wolf pelt onto the stained red cape, Little Red downed another shot, reminding herself that even alcohol has a better taste than the gastric acid of a wolf.— Rahul Kak, Ann Arbor, MI

Jacob and Elisa had been warned by their parents on numerous occasions never to venture into the Amber Woods after dark or risk some vague and unspoken fate once within the trees, so they didn't and just played in their front yards instead.— Eric Lorenz, Phoenix, AZ

Winner, Crime/Detective:
John thought of Kate and smiled--with any luck the tide would carry her body out to deeper water by nightfall. — Tom Billings, Minneapolis, MN

Runner-Up, Crime/Detective:
When the corpse showed up in the swimming pool, her dead bosoms bobbing up and down like twin poached eggs in hollandaise sauce, Randy decided to call the police as soon as he finished taking pictures of his breakfast and posting them to his Facebook wall. — Laura Ruth Loomis, Pittsburg, CA

Dishonorable Mentions, Crime/Detective:
I knew that dame was damaged goods when she first sauntered in, and I don't mean lightly scratched and dented goods that a reputable merchant like Home Depot might offer in a clearly marked end display sale; no, she was more like the kind of flashy trashy plastic knockoff that always carries a child-choking hazard that no self-respecting 11-year-old Chinese sweat shop kids would ever call theirs. — Tom Billings, Minneapolis, MN

The janitor's body lay just inside the door, a small puncture wound below his right ear made with a long thin screwdriver, the kind electricians use and can often be found in the bargain bin at the hardware store and come with a pair of cheap wire cutters that you never use because they won't cut wire worth a damn and at best will only put a small indent in the wire so you can at least bend it back and forth until it breaks. — E. David Moulton, Summerville, SC

When private detective Flip Merlot spotted the statuesque brunette seated at the bar of his favorite watering hole, he was drawn to her like a yellow cat to navy blue pants, and when he sidled up next to her he felt fuzzy all over, kind of like dark blue corduroys get when they're matted with yellow cat hair. — James M. Vanes, La Porte, IN

Winner, Fantasy:
The three Black Forest Elves, Twinklemann, Sparklemann, and Von Dazzleberg, were sitting at their merry campfire, frying their wursts and hamhocks, slathering their rich black bread with the grease, drinking the icy magical Rhine-water, and one of them at least puffing away on a pudgy little elven-pipe, when who should show up but the OTHER famous elves Oberon, Titania, Galadriel, Elrond, Tinkerbell, the Munchkin lollipop dude, and that thing on the airplane wing in "Twilight Zone." — David S Nelson, Falls Church, VA

Runner-Up, Fantasy:
That was magic alright, though she belatedly realized that she should have known because everybody else was wearing robes while holding staffs with knobs on one end and screaming nonsense like "Merlin's beard!" when she unceremoniously dropped in their midst and it really shouldn't have taken her being changed into a creature of the amphibian persuasion to comprehend that. — Yap Tee Giut, Ipoh, Perak, Malaysia

Dishonorable Mentions, Fantasy:
"My name is Vangir," the stout dwarf announced, "son of Valdir, son of Tolfdir, son of Torsson, heir to the dwarf kingdom of Darag-Vur, King of the Under-Folk, ring-giver, dragon-slayer, M.D., DDS. — Austin Stollhaus, Louisville, KY

An evil darkness strode across the forsaken lands of Marmon, casting a shadow like a superhero whose cape's special power is to turn day into night, that was how the darkness strode (not like the superhero who was otherwise a very nice man). — Terence Mulholland, Santa Monica, CA

In the forest of Thrangul, Dobo Snabeley stared at his quest companions, Bolto Dwaven, Eagle Thepnis, Night Hunter, and Lythan Elva, looking to a map of Husker-Du, Dobo knew they would traverse this entire world to burn the Wand of Shazna in the firepit of Mound Hapla, so Dobo chucked it in the camp fire instead, and went home. — Nad Razvi, Essex, UK

Winner, Historical Fiction:
With his lamp giving off a dull yellow glow General Washington sat up late into the night contemplating his problems: Not enough food, not enough clothing, not enough men, and that idiot Private Doodle who kept putting feathers in his cap and calling it macaroni.— Dan Leyde, Shoreline, WA

Runner-Up, Historical Fiction:
Attila sat alone on the crest of a hill overlooking the bucolic village he would next pillage, envying the simple lives of its denizens, but comforting himself with the knowledge that they would soon all be murdered. — Steve Lerner, Northridge, CA

Dishonorable Mentions, Historical Fiction:
The year was 1792, and the French Royal family was like a well-watered topiary: lush, widespread, and in need of a good pruning. — Arch Robison, Champaign, IL

Winner, Horror:
If Vicky Walters had known that ordering an extra shot of espresso in her grande non-fat sugar free one pump raspberry syrup two pumps vanilla syrup soy latte that Wednesday would lead to her death and subsequent rebirth as a vampire, she probably would have at least gotten whipped cream.— Margo Coffman, Corinth MS

Runner-Up, Horror:
Duane made a very unfortunate zombie; the coroner had removed his dentures and all of his clothes before he reanimated--thus he was destined to stagger naked through the woods, attempting to gum small animals to death.— Stephanie Leanne Myers, Baton Rouge, LA

Winner, Purple Prose:
Carlos stared in lust and amazement as she walked away, her spandex-covered body giving the impression of two well-oiled sumo wrestlers on stilts furiously going for the win. — Marlin Back, Columbus, IN

Runner-Up, Purple Prose:
It was the age of the expected, it was the age of surprises, it was the season of Light, it was the season of Darkness, it was the spring of hope, it was the fall of despair, we had everything before us, we had nothing before us--in short, the period was so different from past periods that some of us didn't know what else to do but go to Las Vegas and drink smoothies. — Ron Johnstone, Burlingame, CA

Dishonorable Mentions, Purple Prose:
Long overdue for a tune-up, the ancient and dilapidated 1956 Oldsmobile -- with PowerGlide transmission and power steering -- wheezed slowly into the gas station, the long, blue plumes of exhaust looking like a crop duster full of illegal DDT spraying a field of asphalt. — Ed Buhrer, Louisa, VA

He typed like a ninja with no arms, and the text flowed like a drop of blood down a katana blade sharpened with one of those automatic kitchen things you can buy on late-night television when you're drunk but not too drunk to read off your 16-digit credit card number and security code.— Alex Dering, Brooklyn, NY

The night was dark; which is a bit redundant, since night is by definition dark, unless it's a stormy night when lightning causes moments of brilliant light, or except in places like Norway or Alaska where summer nights can be pretty light, but still, most of the time when you say "night," people are going to think "dark." — Joseph E. Fountain, Fredericksburg, VA

Portly, abrupt Bart Simeon plodded through the citadel with a bearing of tension and anger that was like a tinderbox lying by a roadside waiting for a careless motorist to toss his or her cigarette butt out the window, most likely the passenger if the container lay on the right side of the road, or perhaps the driver with a brusque flick to the left, unless of course if they were in England, in which case it would be the opposite. — Anthony Hahn, Astoria, OR

She looked like a great pizza, you know the kind that relies more on the quality of the sauce than the amount of cheese, standing there powdering her nose, which was a bit large for her face, reminding him of a slice of pizza whose point curled up after a night in the refrigerator. — Howard Vogl, San Luis Obispo, CA

I never did see the last thing I saw, the truck and the red light, the last thing I saw was a plus-size girl in a petite ensemble, giving her the appearance of a marshmallow tightly wrapped in dental floss. — Ted Wise, Hanover, PA

Winner, Romance:
Claire had more daddy issues than Boy's Life magazine published in the late 1970s, but she was a perfect match for Donald, whose personality was vaguely sticky, like the outside of a squeezable honey container or anything handled by a three-year-old. — James Pokines, Boston, MA

Runner-Up, Romance:
She was a mermaid equally at home on land and water because of her dual-membrane lungs, and she had everything I needed tucked under one beautiful big scale, and her glistening, wriggling, flopping body and melodious Siren's voice had me in love from day one when I hauled her up along with 600 pounds of Point Judith #3 calamari. — David S Nelson, Falls Church VA

Dishonorable Mentions, Romance:
Wilbur's passionate kisses sent a warm shiver down Eugenia's tender spine and made the coarse hair on her knuckles erect. — David Pepper, Torrance, CA

As he caressed her hair, cheek, forehead, chin, collarbone, shoulder, upper arm, and stomach, she knew that her decision to take Octoman as a lover was the correct one. — Lynda Clark, Nottingham, UK

Caitlin was a Pop Tart kind of girl, but Kyle always ate four Aunt Jemima pancakes with Land o' Lakes unsalted butter and Mrs. Butterworth's maple syrup, so they knew they would never marry because of their differences, but they could still fool around. — Kathy Minicozzi, Bronx, NYC

This is a story about love, but not just any kind of love like how you love the feeling of trading in a pair of soggy, old socks for fresh ones, or the taste of salty French fries dipped in a chocolate milkshake, I'm talking about the other kind of love. — Anna Sagstetter, Fort Wayne, IN

Their love had come upon her completely by surprise, thought Amelia -- like when you're looking into your rearview and side mirrors to decide whether it's feasible to switch into the passing lane and you think you're in the clear, but then you find yourself utterly sideswiped. — Allison Sloto, Pottstown, PA

It was debatable what Felicity enjoyed most about the night – the delicious dinner, the marvelous movie, or the satisfying sex – but one thing was clear and that was that she hoped she wouldn't be doing it alone again next time. — Randy Blanton, Murfreesboro, TN

Well . . ." began the mother as she attempted to answer her daughter's question, amid fuzzy memories of a balmy night in Cuba, several empty bottles of pineapple rum lying around the bed she had shared with the Captain accompanied by the worst headache she could remember, "I wouldn't use the word 'accident.'" — Alex Main, Springboro, OH

Camilla was a strong, confident woman who ran a Fortune 500 company and made her own yogurt, but what she really longed for was a control-freak guy who would tap her phone, lock her in her room, and force her to listen to Gilbert Gottfried singing the national anthem. — Laura Ruth Loomis, Pittsburg, CA

Winner, Science Fiction:
The gravitational pull up here on Mars is much less than it is back at home base, of course, so your tongue sticks to the roof of our mouth and everyone sounds like Eleanor Roosevelt. — John Holmes, St. Petersburg, FL

Runner-Up, Science Fiction:
Entering the Forbidden Zone on Planet Q38 Minor meant death, either quickly by mushroom poisoning or terribly by The Shiny Golden Hook; but Captain Zirek didn't care, he was in love with three-legged Zora, and that's where she was stabled. — David S Nelson, Falls Church VA

Dishonorable Mentions, Science Fiction:
Turk strained at the controls of the Pulsar-Phased Adenoid Five Galactic Cruiser, trying desperately to pull up from an uncontrolled dive, until he suddenly remembered he was in space, and there is no up or down. — Joseph E. Fountain, Fredericksburg, VA

The mighty roar of the awesome atomic engines (louder than a thousand MGM lions, more powerful than lust on a warm summer's day) erotically thrust the metallic monster into the heavens like some demonic angel escaping from Hell and made the intrepid astronaut swallow his gum. — James Luce, Los Altos, CA

The Phylognites made love by intertwining their eyeball stalks, a most erotic sensation except occasionally when, due to inexperience or excessive ardor, their stalks became inextricably bound in what (unbeknownst to them) a species of obnoxious, quarrelsome little bipeds on an obscure planet circling a small star in the Milky Way might call a "bird's nest." — Wayne Carmichael, Tyler, TX

Winner, Vile Puns:
Locals know it as Pinocchio Rock, because it's shaped like a proboscis, and lies at the edge of the cliff. — John Holmes, St. Petersburg, FL

Runner-Up, Vile Puns:
Having eaten her fill of the town's fils et filles, the French witch inspected her candy-encrusted house and decided she needed a grander lure to attract grander prey--perhaps she should build a homme depot. — Scott Britton, Boston, MA

Dishonorable Mentions, Vile Puns:
As James King, detective in the Queens branch of the NYPD stared at the rooks pecking at the disheveled corpse of Bishop Robert Knight in the alley behind the pawn shop, he checked for his mates. — Mark McGivern, Albert Lea, MN

Old Man Dracula forgot to put his teeth in one night, and so had to come home hungry, with a sort of "nothing dentured, nothing veined" look on his face.— Matthew Pfeifer Beaman IA

Sherlock Holmes brusquely dismissed his companion's theory that the victim had died from an allergic reaction to either seasoning or seafood, saying "Watson, although the problem is alimentary, it is neither the Thyme nor the Plaice." — Owen Roberts, Edina, MN

Winner, Western:

Spurs a-jangling, Black Bert sauntered to the bar and cried "this town ain't big enough!"—then gulped a whisky, fingered his six-shooter, and belched—"so I say we annex Dry Gulch, thus increasing our tax base while simultaneously reducing fixed costs through economies of scale." — Joel Phillips, West Trenton, NJ

Runner-Up, Western
"Pecos Mac" McCarthy index-fingered back the brim of his battered Stetson, squatted at the edge of the waterhole, cupped a handful of brackish water, squinted out over the shimmering alkali flats of the Badlands, and decided then and there that he had prit' near had it with overwrought, hackneyed western imagery. — Joseph Pramuk, Napa, CA

Miscellaneous Dishonorable Mentions
He tried to drown out her pleas for help by holding her head under the water, but it just wasn't working – her head continuing to bob out of the water like a plastic duck or anything else that's plastic. — Randy Blanton, Murfreesboro, TN

Barnaby asked the counter girl for a pastrami sandwich on rye with heartbreak, onions, and ennui on it, wrapped to go in the soul of a sheep, to which she turned wearily and yelled, "Another number six!"— Jeff Coleburn, West Chester, PA

"You're a dead man, O' Flanagan," said the mortuary supervisor to the corpse laid out before him, chuckling to himself at how comical that remark was, a sentiment not shared with the rest of the night shift who all secretly yearned for the day he retired, having heard the same joke on innumerable occasions with just the surname of the deceased changed. — Ted Downes, Cardiff, U.K.

It was a dark and stormy night, and right there in front of me, she stood, dripping with rainwater beside the white chickens and the red wheelbarrow, her dress ripped and soggy. — Susie Gawriluk, Presque Isle, WI

The perspiration left a gentle sheen on his forehead but this was to his disadvantage because it usually encouraged his McDonald's visor to belly flop into the fry oil and the resultant siphoning, scouring, and replacement of the melted visor goo-fouled fryer oil could really throw off the lunch rush and once again set back his long-overdue corporate mcbump from shift supervisor to assistant manager. — Doc Martian, Indio, CA

It had been a quite a week for Marvin Sturgis; he'd finally accepted a six-figure salary at his dream company, Mattel, the American toy-manufacturer, and was now treating himself to a beautiful dinner, pouring imaginary tea into tiny toy teacups, talking aloud to the five life-size Barbie dolls he'd positioned around his kitchen table, and cursing the shipping company for its inability to transport all six figures at once. — Daniel Ryan, New York City, NY

It was a windy day, the kind where men's greasy ball caps blew off like so many meth cookers exploding on makeshift stoves, or so I've heard (but I don't even drink alcohol, so what do I really know about it? though I have been known to let it all hang out and occasionally harrumph loudly at the stamp counter if someone breaks the queue). — Leigh Ward-Smith, New Douglas, IL

The assassin paired his weapon and victim like the master sommelier he had longed to be since growing up in the still, up-and-coming but not yet fully respected vineyards of the Columbia River Gorge, the afternoon's choice a Glock 38 that bridged the gap between concealment and power providing the smooth finish and light retort appropriate to the crowded open air café, while this evening's mark in the vacant industrial park meriting the full-bodied Magnum with its robust finish and exemplary cordite bouquet. — Clark Snodgrass, Huntington Beach, CA

My mother died when I was nine, my father when I was twelve, which left me somewhat cold, and hardened and unable to love, though I was partial to Nando's Portuguese style prawns. — William Telford, UK

It was time to let the lads loose on the job -- Gonda had been *totally* impossible and he couldn't take any more; so today all ten Rottweilers would be in for a feast and he hoped the forensic investigation wouldn't find any traces of DNA in the back yard. — Edward Vincent Tennant, Edgemead, South Africa

As the giant gorilla swept her up in his hand and started to climb the skyscraper a swarm of fighter biplanes roared overhead and although frightened out of her wits Marjory had a tremendous feeling of deja-vu. — Mal Walker, Mount Barker, South Australia

"I'm nothing without you," Steele Harrison told Mavis Prescott, which was true on many levels, but primarily because he was her imaginary friend. — Tom Wallace Columbia, SC

Beppe Rococo, owner of the largest open-air farmer's market in North Africa, after lovingly filling the arms of the beautiful vegan Taffy, who hailed from a Barcelona bistro, with bunches of fresh kale and organic carrots, breathed in her ear, "Come with me to the quinoa." — Jim Wollak, San Francisco, CA

His parents having just sent him from their Crown Heights neighbourhood to keep him out of the Jewish gangs, Schmuley eyed his seemingly shy classmates on his new working-class elementary school playground in Cedar Rapids and considered taunting them, but he decided it best not yet to toy with the coy goy boy hoi polloi. — Patrick Yamada, Orange, CA

Stephanie did not intend to become an animal coroner when she went to veterinary school, but the workload was manageable and, for cats, she usually just had to check the "curiosity" box under "cause of death."— Doug Purdy, Roseville, CA

He was an old man who fished alone on a skiff in the Gulf Stream and he had gone eighty-four days now without taking a fish, but in the meantime had perfected his killer mojito and opened a beachside bar where patrons now stood three deep waiting to taste his magic at four U.S. bucks a pop. — Ray Clarke, Concord CA

Mother's Day Thanks
By Joan Leotta

Thanks to you,
every day,
every ordinary day
whether graced with sunshine or
laced with rains of sorrow
is good.
Thanks to you,
I see
happiness is from within,
Not without.
Thanks to you.
each day
brings a full measure
of joy
to my life.
Thanks to you.

Sweet mother, I cannot ply the loom, vanquished by a desire and I am longing to be with you." Sappho (c. 612 B.C.)

The Green Thing
Unknown Source

The young cashier suggested to the much older lady that she should bring her own grocery bags, because plastic bags are not good for the environment. The woman apologized to the young girl and explained, "We didn't have this 'green thing' back in my earlier days."

The young clerk responded, "That's our problem today. Your generation did not care enough to save our environment for future generations."

The older lady said that she was right -- our generation didn't have the "green thing" in its day. The older lady went on to explain

"Back then, we returned milk bottles, soda bottles, and beer bottles to the store. The store sent them back to the plant to be washed and sterilized and refilled, so it could use the same bottles over and over. So they really were recycled. But we didn't have the "green thing" back in our day.

"Grocery stores bagged our groceries in brown paper bags that we reused for numerous things. Most memorable, besides household garbage bags, was the use of brown paper bags as book covers for our schoolbooks. This was to ensure that public property (the books provided for our use by the school) was not defaced by our scribbling. Then we were able to personalize our books on the brown paper bags. But, too bad we didn't do the "green thing" back then.

"We walked up stairs because we didn't have an escalator in every store and office building. We walked to the grocery store and didn't climb into a 300-horsepower machine every time we had to go two blocks. But she was right. We didn't have the "green thing" in our day.

"Back then we washed the baby's diapers because we didn't have the throw away kind. We dried clothes on a line, not in an energy-gobbling machine burning up 220-volts. Wind and solar power really did dry our clothes back in our early days. Kids got hand-me-down clothes from their brothers or sisters, not always brand-new clothing. But that young lady is right; we didn't have the "green thing" back in our day.

"Back then, we had one TV, or radio, in the house -- not a TV in every room. And the TV had a small screen the size of a handkerchief (remember them?), not a screen the size of the state of Montana. In the kitchen, we blended and stirred by hand because we didn't have electric machines to do everything for us. When we packaged a fragile item to send in the mail, we used wadded up old newspapers to cushion it, not Styrofoam or plastic bubble wrap. Back then, we didn't fire up an engine and burn gasoline just to cut the lawn. We used a push mower that ran on human power. We exercised by working so we didn't need to go to a health club to run on treadmills that operate on electricity. But she's right; we didn't have the "green thing" back then.

"We drank from a fountain when we were thirsty instead of using a cup or a plastic bottle every time we had a drink of water. We refilled writing pens with ink instead of buying a new pen, and we replaced the razor blade in a razor instead of throwing away the whole razor just because the blade got dull. But we didn't have the "green thing" back then.

"Back then, people took the streetcar or a bus and kids rode their bikes to school or walked instead of turning their moms into a 24-hour taxi service in the family's $45,000 SUV or van, which cost what a whole house did before the "green thing." We had one electrical outlet in a room, not an entire bank of sockets to power a dozen appliances. And we didn't need a computerized gadget to receive a signal beamed from satellites 23,000 miles out in space in order to find the nearest burger joint.

"But isn't it sad that the current generation laments how wasteful we old folks were just because we didn't have the "green thing" back then?

"We don't like being old in the first place, so it doesn't take much to tick us off... especially from a tattooed, multiple-pierced smart-aleck who can't make change without the cash register telling her how much!

A New Year at the Sunset Lodge
Marry Williamson

At the Sunset Lodge, the Christmas celebrations were well and truly over. Things had settled down and to be honest, the days dragged. January, February, March being such boring months everybody was looking forward to the spring. Things were looking up, however, when Mrs. Hartnell came in and announced the advent of a new resident. A Mr. Partridge. First name MacKenzie. Mr. MacKenzie Partridge. "A Partridge in a pear tree" came loud and clear from Norman on the upstairs landing. "How did he know?" Mrs. Hartnell frowned. "He must have overheard the telephone conversation I had with Mr. Partridge's daughter." She turned to the assembled company in the lounge "I want you all on your best behavior. Mr. Partridge is only having a trial stay. See if he likes it here. No funny business and keep that cat in that bag."

Margery, who had been reading 'Company of Liars', put down her book. "Trial stay, indeed. What if we don't like *him*? Still, at least it is a man. It is getting too girlie in here. We can't count on Norman. I hope Mr. Partridge still has all his marbles.

After lunch, just as they were all nicely nodding off over their coffees, the doorbell went. Margery looked out of the window. "Well whoever is bringing him has a nice car" she said approvingly eyeing up the large Mercedes parked out front. There was a murmuring in the hallway and then the door opened and Mrs. Hartnell ushered in a large man of around 80 years of age. Well preserved with a large bluff face, lots of flowing silvery hair and hands like red hams. He was dressed very dapperly in old- fashioned flannels, a blue check shirt and a dark blue blazer with a crest of some sorts on the breast pocket. A red paisley scarf was knotted jauntily round his throat. Everybody was impressed. An elegant middle aged lady followed in his wake. "Well Dad. Here you are. And…. as we discussed, on your best behavior! We don't want any repetition of the last time!" Mr. Partridge turned round: "You still here, Felicity. Why don't you buzz off." There was a sharp intake of breath from the assembled ladies in the room at this rudeness. After the introductions were made Felicity did indeed buzz off without a backward glance at her father. "Well, thank goodness for that" Mr. Partridge said. He looked round the room and smiled a large toothy smile. He had impossible white teeth. "Dentures," Margery said later. "Call me Mac," Mr. Partridge said and grinned widely, the light bouncing off his teeth. From the hallway, Norman could be heard singing: "Oh, the shark has pretty teeth, dear, and he shows them, pearly white." "Who is that?" Mac frowned. "Only Norman, he is not quite ... Alzheimer's," Margery explained. "He likes to sing." Mac shrugged. He looked round the room and went to sit on the little sofa next to Eleanor. He roughly shoved the carpetbag containing George onto the floor ,which elicited an angry cry from the cat. "Cat," Margery offered. "That is George. In the bag." Mac looked puzzled. "Why is he in the bag?" "Don't ask" Margery said. After Mac had pleasantly enquired what Eleanor was reading and had admired Maud and Violet's knitting and quilting efforts it was time for tea. Prudence came in rattling the teatrolly. Apart from the tea urn and cups there was a large fruit loaf baked by Prudence herself. Mac eyed it avidly. "Bread" he said. "Fruit bread. Lovely. And with that he produced a large knife from his blazer pocket and before Prudence, or indeed, anybody else could bat an eyelid he had got up and cut a large slice of the bread. All in one fluid movement. From the hallway came the second verse of Mac the Knife: "Oh, a jack knife, has MacHeath dear and he keeps it out of sight." The room sat in silence. Prudence doled out the tea and slices of fruit loaf, backed out the trolley and disappeared. Mac, meanwhile, wiped his knife on a paper napkin and put it back in his pocked. "I like knives," he said. "I like knives and cutting things," He looked round the room. "What's with you all? Cat's got your tongues?" He opened Eleanor's carpetbag. "Hey George. Got their tongues?" Eleanor looked at him horrified and snatched the bag away from Mac. "Leave him alone," she hissed. "OK lady, keep your hair on. I was only joking." Mac made as if to grab in his blazer pocket again. Just then, Mrs. Hartnell came in followed by Prudence. "Can I have that knife, Mr. Partridge? I don't allow my guests to carry knives. Mac took the knife out of his blazer pocket and took aim. It whizzed past Mrs. Hartnell and Prudence, missing them narrowly and stuck in the door jamb where it stood trembling for a while. The room sat frozen, their mouth perfect O's. Mac looked round the room with satisfaction. Haven't lost it, have I? Best knife thrower in the business, I was. Nobody better."

Barely half an hour later, the Mercedes pulled up and Felicity came in, summoned by Mrs. Hartnell. "Well done, Dad. This time your stuff is not even unpacked. We'll be running out of old folk's homes soon." On the upstairs landing, Norman was finishing Mac the Knife. "On the sidewalk, Sunday morning, lies a body, oozing…." "SHUT UP, NORMAN," They all shouted in unison.

After Felicity had driven Mac off the premises in the big Mercedes, peace and quiet again settled on the Sunset Lodge. Norman had been given two of his little yellow pills and taken to his room. Violet had resumed quilting the little pram cover for Janey's baby, Poppy and Maud's knitting needles were once again clicking. The pale green outfit for Poppy was taking shape. Margery had resumed reading 'Company of Liars' mumbling under her breath about the girl with the runes and all the rain. Eleanor had taken up her magazine and was engrossed in the horoscope page, George in the carpetbag by her side. The Sunset Lodge was back to normal. Until suddenly Eleanor cried out, "Oh, oh, listen to this. My stars. They predict a surprise. It is going to be *my special day.* Tomorrow!" "Special day for what?" Maud looked up from her knitting with a frown. "Pigs, you made me drop a stitch." Violet snorted derisively, and picked another bit of material out of the heap in her basket and smoothed it flat on her knee. Margery did not even look up from her book but commented: "Who believes in that rubbish." "I do. Me and George, we believe it. Don't we, Georgie." Eleanor cooed into the big carpetbag. She put the bag on the floor and clapped her hands together like a seal. "I am so excited. Something *nice* is going to happen. Maybe George can finally be set free. Now *that* would be a *special day!*" "Oh, don't count on that." Margery said. "That is never going to happen." But Eleanor went up to bed that night in a heightened state of excitement, George in the bag clasped under her arm.

The next day dawned cold but sunny. Eleanor was the first one down for breakfast. She was still bubbling with excitement. Nothing happened. Coffee time came and went and apart from the appearance of some flapjacks, baked by Prudence herself with their coffee nothing out of the ordinary happened. They never had flapjacks with their coffee. "And I hope, never again," Margery said. "Hate the bloody things. Stick to your teeth." Even Norman did not like them very much. At least the flapjacks prompted him to burst out in an off-key rendition of 'Hit the road, Jack'. Lunchtime came and went. Nothing.

But then, in the afternoon, a big lorry turned up. It backed into the drive. Two burly men got out and rattled up the back door and started to haul out a couple of big cardboard boxes. The company in the lounge was transfixed, the knitting needles stilled, the quilting dropped back in the basket and even Margery put her book down. Eleanor was beside herself. "See, see, something is happening!" Norman drifted into the lounge singing 'Memories' at the top of his voice. He was followed in by Mrs. Hartnell who frowned, took him by the arm, and hissed: "You've been eavesdropping again, Norman, shut up." Margery looked at them suspiciously. "What does that mean? What does he mean 'memories'?" Mrs. Hartnell shrugged. "You will all find out soon. It is a surprise. You will like it." She left the lounge, taking Norman with her.

They were agog. The two burly men started dragging the big boxes up the stairs into the little box room at the end of the landing that had been empty for as long as all of them could remember. They all took turns to see if they could find out what was happening but the door was closed. Norman could still be heard singing 'memories' but softer and slower until he faded away completely. Mrs. Hartnell had given him a couple of his yellow pills. The speculations in the lounge were rife. Suggestions ranged from a film room to a WiFi machine. When Prudence came in with the tea, she was besieged but she feigned ignorance. "You'll just have to wait," she said.

59

Eventually, as with all these things, there was an end to the waiting. After a couple of hours knocking and banging the two burly men came clattering down the stairs, went out, and stuck a big pole in the middle of the lawn and nailed a board to it. Then they climbed back into the van and disappeared down the drive. As the board was turned towards the road, they could not see what was on it. Just then, Mrs. Hartnell called them all upstairs. She stood smiling in the doorway of the little room and with a wide sweep of her arms invited them in. "Ta-ra," she said excitedly. They all stood frozen, Violet and Maud openmouthed, Margery frowning, and Eleanor with George in the bag under her arm aghast. The little room had been got up to resemble a 1950s corner shop, complete with counter, weighing scales, tins of things long forgotten, and bars of sunlight soap. Even Margery was dumbstruck, her sharp tongue failing her for once. They milled about in the 'shop' aimlessly, picking up this and that, too confused to comment on the items. "Why? What is it all for?" Margery asked but Mrs. Hartnell had already disappeared down the stairs. Prudence came to look and clapped her hands together but did not offer an explanation.

All was revealed, however, when they all trooped into the front garden to see what was on the board. It read, 'We are offering Senior Living with a Neighbourhood Facility for the Memory Impaired'.

The Sunset Lodge was buzzing after the installation of the Neighbourhood Facility for the Memory Impaired. There was even a feature in the local newspaper. All of it much to the disapproval of Margery. She was very vocal about her grievances. "Why do we need this? Now we will be getting the families of all the loonies and fruitcakes wanting their old parents to stay here. Memory Impaired indeed. Alzheimer's more like. We've got Norman. Isn't that enough?" For once Violet, Maud, and Eleanor backed her up. "What we need is people who can still play a decent hand of bridge. People with all their marbles in the right order. It is hard enough coping with Norman." Norman could be heard in the hallway singing, 'Half a pound of tupenny rice, half a pound of treacle'. "See," Margery said. "I rest my case." Eleanor explained: "He has been weighing out things in the neighbourhood facility, playing 'shopkeepers' bless him." "Oh well," Margery said. Let's hope weasel did not hear him," at which both Maud and Violet looked bemused and Eleanor laughed. She tucked George in the carpetbag firmer under her arm and gave it a little squeeze. A loud purring could be heard from within. "He is getting used to being in there" she said to Margery. Margery looked guilty and embarrassed. She was well aware that she was the cause of George being in there and the stumbling block of him being allowed out. Eleanor being so *nice* to her made it awkward. She gave her a little half-smile and said "good." She was about to say something more when Prudence appeared with the tea trolley, which had developed a squeaking wheel, with the tea and a large plate with apple turnovers. Norman appeared in the lounge. "Apple turnthings. My favourite." He took two, one in each hand and disappeared into the hall with them, biting into them alternatively, applesauce dripping down his hands and arms. For once, he was not singing.

Prudence poured out the tea and said, "He has been weighing out things in the 'facility'." She had put the teapot down and made a double-handed sign with two fingers around the word 'facility'. "He wants to make apple turnovers from scratch. I don't like him in the kitchen. What is wrong with Tesco's anyway. But Mrs. Hartnell says it might do him good, 'therapeutic' and all that. She again made two inverted comma signs with her fingers. Maud and Violet nodded: "Ah bless." Eleanor catching Margery's rolled her eyes. Margery biting into her turnover mumbled, "rubbish, just give him another yellow pill." "Wish I could." Prudence sighed squeaking out of the lounge with her trolley.

The 'big apple turnover disaster' as it went down into the annals of the Sunset Lodge happened the next day. Actually on the same day as 'Margery's big turnaround'. Norman had been in a heightened state of excitement weighing out flour and things in the kitchen, singing at the top of his voice 'half a pound of tuppenny rice, half a pound of treacle'. He had cored and peeled a large pan full of apples and set them to cook on Prudence's aga. He had added at least a kilo of sugar to the apple mix and an enormous quantity of cinnamon. The whole thing was bubbling away on the range, large blobs splatting out of the pan and burning onto Prudence's pristine aga. He had made the dough and rolled it out on a large pastry board ready to take the apple mixture. Prudence was by now mewling with frustration and fled into the hallway, her eyes full of tears. Maud, Violet, Margery, and Eleanor were all googly-eyed watching the proceedings from the kitchen doorway. Mrs. Hartnell, whose idea the whole thing was, was nowhere to be seen.

Norman deciding that the apple concoction was ready took the pan off the hob. It was so heavy he had to use both hands. He slopped the stuff onto the dough and roughly rolled it over. Hot apple sauce flew everywhere. He slapped the whole thing onto a big metal turkey tin and stuffed it into the microwave oven. Bits of dough and apple scattered all over the kitchen. Prudence, by now quite hysterical, shouted: "No Norman, not the microwave" but it was too late. Norman had pressed the button. There was a tremendous arcing and a loud bang. The microwave blew up, the big turnover exploded within and the bits caught fire. Prudence fled into the hallway yelling, "Mrs. Hartnell, Mrs. Hartnell." Violet stood wringing her hands, Maud flew into the lounge rescuing her knitting, Eleanor squeezing George safely in the bag under her arm phoned the fire brigade while Margery led Norman upstairs to his room and his yellow pills. He was singing: 'Penny Lane' something about the fireman and his clean machine.

When Mrs. Hartnell returned from town where she had been shopping, it was all over. The kitchen was in ruins but the rest of the house had been spared. Prudence had calmed down and Maud and Violet were quietly quilting and knitting in their customary places by the fire.

But some good came out of the disastrous episode. Well, two things really. One was that Margery at last allowed George out of the bag. "Perhaps we should give him a trial period," she suggested. "See how he goes, poor thing. He can't stay in that ridiculous carpetbag forever." Eleanor, who did not care too much about her bag being called ridiculous (it had been a gift from a grateful parent) swallowed the insult and gave Margery a dazzling smile. "Thank you, dear, very kind," she said. "I am sure George will behave himself impeccably." The other was that for the next few days, until the kitchen had been re-decorated, they were all allowed turns to decide on their favourite take-away meals.

Advice from a Pessimist
Unknown Source

1. Do not walk behind me, for I may not lead. Do not walk ahead of me, for I may not follow. Do not walk beside me for the path is narrow. In fact, just leave me alone.
2. No one is listening until you pass gas.
3. Always remember you're unique. Just like everyone else.

4. Never test the depth of the water with both feet.
5. If you think nobody cares whether you're alive or dead, try missing a couple of payments.
6. Before you criticize someone, you should walk a mile in their shoes. That way, when you criticize them, you're a mile away and you have their shoes.
7. If at first you don't succeed, skydiving is not for you.
8. Give a man a fish and he will eat for a day. Teach him how to fish, and he will sit in a boat and drink beer all day.
9. If you lend someone 20 bucks and never see that person again, it was probably well worth it.
10. If you tell the truth, you don't have to remember anything.
11. Some days you are the dog, some days you are the tree.
12. Good judgment comes from bad experience ... And most of that comes from bad judgment.
    A closed mouth gathers no foot.
13. There are two excellent theories for arguing with women. Neither one of them works.
14. Generally speaking, you aren't learning much when your lips are moving.
15. When you are dead, you don't know that you are dead. It's difficult only for others. It is the same when you are stupid.

A Forgotten Landscape
Ariana Mangum
Chapter 71
Mrs. Haunch's Last Appearance

September 1943

In September, Alvira Carthage's sister died suddenly, the result of a heart attack. Mr. Houghton heard it at Henley's store, and Mrs. Houghton read it in the newspaper. I'd met this lady only once or twice at the Red Cross store when she came with Mrs. Carthage to help us meet our quota. She also had red hair and was worse than her sister for gossip.

The day the obituary came out in the paper Mrs. Haunch called us on the telephone to get information about the funeral.

"It's to be at St. Mary's for some reason because she never went there as far as I can remember," Mrs. Houghton told the hermit. "Yes, ten o'clock on Saturday."

"It's strange Dr. Price would allow Alvira's sister to be buried from a church she never attended," I remarked. "Why is Mrs. Haunch so interested?"

"She knew her. Apparently they attended school together," Mrs. Houghton replied. "I don't know all the answers, but Mrs. Haunch wants to come."

"That's strange," I said, "she never goes any place except when there is a fire or some sort of crisis."

"I expect she considers this a crisis," Mrs. Houghton went into the kitchen to prepare our supper which she always called tea.

On Saturday we drove to St. Mary's through a hot summer haze. The countryside seemed lifeless as the sultry humidity enveloped it like a cloak. White dust choked the grass along the roadside. This heavy atmosphere made me feel depressed, and Jackie jogged along slowly feeling listless. My spirits sank as we arrived at St. Mary's Church. All our neighbors were there looking hot and unhappy in the breathless morning humidity.

Catherine Hollis met us at the church steps and spoke in a whisper. Mrs. Carthage arrived carrying her fan, compliments of Bennett's Funeral Parlor. I noticed it was a new one to replace her usual Sunday one, which was in tatters. Colonel Hollis escorted her in and placed her in the front pew. He still limped from his wound, but was better. In fact, he was working part-time again.

I noticed Alvira Carthage looked especially nice all in white with a big straw hat that hid her red hair. She sat alone in her pew; apparently, her husband wasn't coming.

"He didn't like the sister," Colonel whispered when he returned to the church door and led us up the aisle near the front. He knew we always sat there so Mrs. Houghton could hear.

I watched as the neighbors gathered. Mrs. Taliaferro arrived with her two daughters. She looked beautiful as always in her elegant light blue dress. She nodded to me as she took her seat behind us. Mrs. Armstrong came and sat beside me. Her cheeks had their usual round circles of rouge, but she wore a pretty, yellow-flowered dress. She picked up my hand and gave it a friendly squeeze. Dorothy and Lizzie took their places, one at the organ, the other next to her mother. Mrs. Armstrong took out her fan and handed it to me. Then she gave a second to Mrs. Houghton. After seeing us looked after, she opened a third fan, painted with lovely Chinese scenes, and began to move the humid air around us. Lizzie started the music and sounded as if she'd practiced some this week in preparation because she hit no wrong notes.

"Abide with me, fast fall the evening tide"

When we sang this hymn, I thought the music sounded better than usual. Dorothy, I noticed, wasn't singing, so the rest of us were on key. I wondered if she had a cold. Surely Dr. Price had not told her to be quiet. He was difficult, but not to the point that he was rude.

Suddenly a great silence fell over the church. At first I thought it was out of respect for Alvira Carthage. I turned around and watched, fascinated, as Mrs. Haunch hobbled up the aisle. She was clad in a teal blue dress, red high heels, and a straw hat trimmed with crimson cherries. She appeared unable to walk in the high heels as she came down the aisle towards us. In her hand she carried a bright red pocket-book and grey gloves. I couldn't believe my eyes, and neither could the congregation. Every head in the church turned towards Mrs. Haunch.

"Look who's here," I nudged Mrs. Houghton.

Mrs. Houghton made no sign and appeared busy with the service. I squirmed around in my seat and stared. Mrs. Taliaferro had her handkerchief pressed against her mouth. Jean and Sally Anne had tears running down their cheeks. Mrs. Armstrong's shoulders shook, and I knew she was silently laughing. Mrs. Hollis looked amazed by this apparition as it made its way into the front pew and sat beside Alvira Carthage.

"I guess if you wear jodhpurs all the time, you don't know how to dress for the public," I whispered to Mrs. Houghton.

"Quite extraordinary," she whispered back.

I watched Mrs. Haunch open her hymnal, putting her finger to her lips before she turned the pages. Lizzie hit a strong chord and we all started the second verse, forgetting where we had left off.

"Stop wiggling," Mrs. Houghton said to me as I leaned over the pew to see this most unusual sight. "You are acting like a child, it's not polite."

I was not trying to act like anything else. I considered myself half child, half woman - some days, all woman - on others, all child. I wondered if I ever would learn to be as composed as Mrs. Taliaferro. Her dress was unwrinkled, her straw-hat fit perfectly, I heard her clear voice behind me singing the hymn. I envied her, she was everything I thought a true lady should be.

I noticed that Mrs. Armstrong had dropped her fan onto the floor in front of us. Quietly I leaned over to pick it up. My eyes met Mrs. Haunch's as she reached under her pew. I nodded politely, then saw that she was sitting in the front row in her stocking feet. Her red shoes had vanished. Mrs. Houghton noticed this too and suppressed a laugh. I dared not look at her because floods of giggles would escape me. I stared at Dr. Price, hoping just looking at his ugly face would sober me.

It didn't help much. It was a great relief when the service was finally over.

I watched as Mrs. Taliaferro, with her daughters, walked down the aisle like a goddess, her clear brown eyes regarded me as she smiled. I nodded back. I knew her emotions were under firm control because although she saw Mrs. Haunch's stocking feet, Mrs. Taliaferro showed no sign of knowing even when Alvira Carthage slipped out a side door and left her friend still sitting in the front pew. Mrs. Taliaferro was every inch a lady and I watched as her stately figure left the church.

Furtively I stole a glance at Mrs. Haunch. She stood in the pew, clad in her strange costume and no shoes. With the utmost dignity, an older man whom I didn't know handed back the red high heels. I watched Mrs. Haunch put them on. Very gently, Mrs. Houghton placed her hand upon my shoulder as a signal for me to move forward. With great reluctance, I walked slowly down the aisle in front of her, and we left the church.

That was the last time I ever say Mrs. Haunch, although she telephoned us from time to time. She went back into her house with her forty-two dogs and James, who came often to Henley's store to buy sacks of dog food.

Letters

September 1943
Richmond, Va.

Dear Dad,
Mrs. Haunch came out of Ballyclare and caused a sensation in church. Mrs. Carthage's sister died suddenly of a heart attack and we all went to the funeral. Mrs. Haunch came in late wearing bright red shoes and a hat with cherries. Can you believe it - cherries for a funeral? Then to top it all off she took offher shoes and lost them. It must have offended the Lord considerably since it was a very hot day. Her shoes disappeared right under her pew, and some gentleman retrieved them for her after the service. If I took off my shoes I'd surely get hell from Mrs. Houghton.

How insulting to the Almighty. He must be furious. It's the talk of the county from the Court House to Tuckahoe Creek.

I hear you are in England. Where are you? Cary is there also with the 8<h Air Force. He's flying on missions. That's scary, but he loves it. How far is Cary from you? Perhaps you can visit him.

Love, Doc

P.S. About God. I've decided that I'll learn more about Him as you suggested. Anyway, I like the music and I like seeing the people I know. I could give up Dr. Price's sermons tomorrow, but we are stuck with him for the duration. I like teaching Sunday school too, but I'd like God to hear me. Mary is better about that, but God often is deaf even when I shout. Mr. Houghton says that's not polite to shout at God. It makes Him angry.

Doc

Continued Next Issue

Who Was Franklin Delano Roosevelt?
Peggy Ellis

Throughout childhood, I thought of our fourth month in terms of pranks and rain. I outgrew the pranks and, at some point, stopped saying "rain, rain go away, come again another day." As an adult, I've had to deal with taxes – worse than rain any day.

However, over the past few months, my thoughts on April have turned to President Franklin Delano Roosevelt, the only person who won four elections to the White House.

After my brother passed away in June, my nephew and I cleared the home place of many years accumulation of stuff, valuable to others perhaps at one time, but not to us now.

The farmhouse, built in 1902, has a cellar, not a basement. On this particular day, I sat at the kitchen table sorting through papers while Dean dealt with the junk in the cellar. He came in, cobwebs clinging to his Atlanta Braves cap, and set a Kerr canning jar on the table. He'd found it on a shelf and wanted to know what it was. The contents were not recognizable, but, suddenly, I was back in time to April 12, 1945.

My brown hair was in braids, a pair of wire-rimmed glasses perched on my nose. I wore new tan corduroy overalls, a white blouse with puffed sleeves, bobby sox, and saddle shoes, the first I'd ever owned. That made me a big girl. Some things are unforgettable.

I skipped at my mom's heels as she hurried from the kitchen to the porch. There I stared at her, my mouth gaped open, as she called to my dad to come in. "Right now," she yelled. He wrapped the horse's reins around the plow handles and came at a run, calling all the way, "What's wrong, what's wrong?"

"Roosevelt died," she told him, her voice as solemn as I'd ever heard it. "How will we ever manage now?"

I was seven years old and didn't have a clue who Roosevelt was, but I did have some understanding of someone dying. My paternal grandfather had died less than a year before, and my maternal grandmother had been dead only a few weeks. Death meant sadness. Death meant

65

tiptoeing around while Mom and Dad fought tears. Death meant we wouldn't see that person again.

I have no recollection of my siblings being there. It was a Thursday, a school day, so why was I at home? Illness, perhaps, although I don't recall ever being ill as a child.

I leaned against Daddy's chair as the man on the radio repeated the news. This person named Roosevelt had died of a massive stroke some place in Georgia, wherever that was. When that serious voice stopped for a commercial, I clamored to know who had died. They ignored me as they sat in stunned silence for what seemed like forever.

"What's going to happen now?" my mom asked. "He pulled us through the depression, but what about the war? Will somebody stop it now? Will Bob come home?"

Bob was my daredevil oldest brother who had joined the Navy the moment Dad agreed to sign for him.

Dad simply shook his head at Mom's question, and after a while returned to plowing the garden.

The only other thing I remember about that day was my mom filling quart jars with a wild salad green called crow's foot and putting them in the hot water canner. I possibly remember that only in hindsight because Dad never allowed her to open the last jar.

Life returned to normal for us on that little farm in the mountains of North Carolina after the immediate upset caused by FDR's death. This person who had died wasn't someone I knew, someone who had shared our supper table, so his death didn't affect me. Or did it?

Hindsight tells me it did. When Roosevelt died, Harry-the buck-stops-here-Truman became president. Only three months thereafter, Truman ordered the atomic bomb dropped in Japan, followed quickly by the Japanese surrender thereby ending the war. That, in turn, meant Bob had survived more than two years on board ships in the Pacific and would now come home. Mom would no longer watch helplessly as the mail carrier passed our house without leaving a letter from him, sometimes for weeks on end. When Mom didn't worry, I didn't either. So, yes, the death of FDR did affect me.

Would Roosevelt have ordered the bombing? Would the man my parents had variously described as compassionate, humane, and caring have been able to order the death of innocent people?

Possibly, even probably, since he had ordered the bomb to be developed. Truman's act stopped the mindless slaughter the Japanese were carrying out against their own people as well as those of the United States and our allies. Still, knowing in theory what could happen and seeing the reality of it are two entirely different things.

Perhaps FDR's death came at the right time, thereby allowing this compassionate man to avoid knowing of the destruction of Hiroshima and Nagasaki.

However, was FDR really compassionate, or was he the warmonger some people called him? Did he deliberately ignore intelligence warnings about a Japanese attack on Pearl Harbor in order to involve us in the war that was devastating so much of the world? The war, by the way, that Congress had refused to allow us to enter despite FDR's efforts.

I suppose who this wheelchair-bound man really was will always be a matter of opinion. For some people, he was the man who single-handedly pulled this nation through a devastating decade of deprivation. For others, he was the monster who sent so many of our young men to their deaths on foreign soil. There were others, my parents included, who rejoiced in his efforts throughout the depression, but ranted when their sons marched off to war.

Whatever or whoever he was, his death affected everybody worldwide in one way or another.

I explained this to Dean. He picked up the jar and returned it to its place on the dusty shelf in the cellar. It will probably remain there another 70 years.

Augustine: Conversions to Confessions
Robin Lane Fox
Reviewed by E. B. Alston

This is a well-researched new account of Augustine up to the time the Confessions were dictated in 397. Not much is known about Augustine of Hippo (354-430 A.D.), who is famous as saint, doctor of the Church, and the greatest of the Church Fathers. He made sense of the doctrine of original sin, the logic that connects mankind's eternal fate to offenses in the Garden of Eden. He wrote that sex is a mammoth obstacle to a Christian life. His life's mission came to him in a garden, when he heard a child's voice from nearby chanting, "Pick it up, read it!" He picked up and read a command in Paul of Tarsus's letters to leave his dissolute life behind.

Saint Augustine's achievements the next forty years as a moral, intellectual, and institutional authority were foundational. They seem so because they were almost pitifully unlikely to happen amid the upheavals of late antiquity. They look like strange interludes containing huge blanks in the record of his life. He "converted" without knowing anything about monastic communities or the Nicene Creed, which was a ritual secret. His journey to Truth is strewn with periods of brilliant confusion, and pragmatic readjustments. But always there was this hyper-concentrated intelligence which had a passionate love of God.

He was a haloed theologian on the one hand and a ruthless ascetic whose prevailing images are less interesting than the man we get to know in Fox's account.

If God could do all this with a hormone-fogged, smart-aleck, self-pitying, lower-middle-class boy from North Africa, during one of civilization's tumultuous, least propitious, eras for doing anything with anyone, what couldn't He do?

Augustine spent his early years as a subordinate "hearer" in Manichaean literature and practice of this nominally Christian sect. Explaining his understanding about Manichaean beliefs in the Confessions is a daunting scholarly task. It seems a lot like mastering multiple versions of Scientology's Dianetics in some old unused language. Then laying out the entire mythology and ritual, along with their background, for ordinary readers.

Fox's explanation of the religion Mani founded is eloquent. It was a major influence on the young Augustine. He describes a hilarious episode; a scandal mentioned in Confessions. It occurred about the time Augustine became sole bishop of Hippo. It seems there were false rumors that he had played an obscene cultic prank on two rich, pious, church officials in Italy. They were pretenders who were founding a religious community with their vast wealth.

Libanius (c. 314-c. 392), was a lifelong pagan, a contemporary of Augustine, was of aristocratic heritage, and a Greek literary scholar. On all these counts, he would have despised the obscurely striving, Latin-speaking, and hopeless Greek-hating Augustine, born to a Christian mother and marked instantly for the catechumenate (the period in advance of baptism). Both were rhetoricians, and thus members of a profession very important to ancient culture and education under the Roman Empire.

City chairs of rhetoric were public offices. Libanius held the one at Antioch, and Augustine the one at Milan before renouncing this possible path to imperial administrative heaven. Moreover, Libanius, like Augustine, wrote an astonishing amount, including a summary of his life with arguments about its meaning. Independent of ideology, a sufficient sense of the private self made such an undertaking conceivable by this time. The idea of a private self for everyone, including women and slaves, in the sense that we understand it was new at the time.

Synesius (c. 373-c. 414) was a fellow Christian bishop in North Africa and a striking example of the divided world Augustine occupied. He was a wealthy and prominent diplomat, a tireless hunter, and a brave military leader. He allowed himself to be drafted as a Christian cleric, with the stipulation that his lifestyle would not change. He would even continue to have sex with his wife. In technically the same church, Augustine felt guilty even gazing with interest at a dog chasing a hare in a field, and lobbied a former protégé against marriage and a secular career as a parent today would lobby against their child selling drugs.

Both Synesius and Augustine shared a calling to pagan philosophy. Synesius had studied with the great Hypatia. During his late adolescence, Augustine was enflamed with idealism, not by the Bible, whose crude style in Latin he despised when he finally confronted it. He still had the standard pagan high-literary schooling, based on Cicero's Hortensius, which was a dialogue about the glories of philosophy.

Augustine delayed his "catholic" baptism partly because of excruciating doubts about the "substance" of God and related philosophical preoccupations. His struggle for celibacy was not because of Christian rules, but because his pious mother, Monica, wanted him to refrain from the romantic entanglements and damage his career in the church. He finally sneaked away from her to Italy. Pure contemplation was on one side, and on the other was the animalistic life of physical sensation and practical activity.

The words of the Jewish Paul that he read in the garden echoed basic, long-established, rules against illicit sex. This had little or nothing to do with worldview. Augustine completed the link over the decades to come. He made poetic, emotionally appealing, but theoretically weak links between the Bible and his inner needs and the Church's outer ones. His greatest achievement subsisted in the overall movement from airless abstraction to populist religion. This movement was instigated because he was an active cleric. As any cleric will agree, nothing works with a congregation except the evidence that you love them. Augustine's great gift of love to us was his words.

Black & White TV
Unknown Source

Whoever wrote it could have been my next door neighbor because it totally described my childhood to a 'T.' Under age 45? You won't understand.

Black and White TV: You could hardly see the picture for all the snow, spread the rabbit ears as far as they go.

Before the news got mean, it was, "Good Night, David." "Good Night, Chet."

My Mom used to cut chicken, chop eggs, and spread mayo on the same cutting board with the same knife and no bleach, but we didn't get food poisoning.

My Mom used to defrost hamburger on the counter and I used to eat it raw sometimes, too. Our school sandwiches were wrapped in wax paper in a brown paper bag, not in ice pack coolers, but I can't remember getting e.coli.

Almost all of us would have rather gone swimming in the lake instead of a pristine pool (talk about boring), no beach closures then.

The term cell phone would have conjured up a phone in a jail cell, and a pager was the school PA system.

We all took gym, not PE ... and risked permanent injury with a pair of high top Ked's (only worn in gym) instead of having cross-training athletic shoes with air cushion soles and built in light reflectors. I can't recall any injuries but they must have happened because they tell us how much safer we are now.

Flunking gym was not an option ... even for stupid kids! I guess PE must be much harder than gym.

Speaking of school, we all said prayers and sang the national anthem, and staying in detention after school caught all sorts of negative attention.

We must have had horribly damaged psyches. What an archaic health system we had then. Remember school nurses? Ours wore a hat and everything.

I thought that I was supposed to accomplish something before I was allowed to be proud of myself.

I just can't recall how bored we were without computers, Play Station, Nintendo, X-box or 270 digital TV cable stations.

Oh yeah ... and where was the Benadryl and sterilization kit when I got that bee sting?

I could have been killed!

But wasn't.

We played 'king of the hill' on piles of gravel left on vacant construction sites, and when we got hurt, Mom pulled out the 48-cent bottle of Mercurochrome. We kids liked it better because it didn't sting like iodine did. Then we got our butt spanked.

Now it's a trip to the emergency room, followed by a 10-day dose of a $99 bottle of antibiotics, and then Mom calls the attorney to sue the contractor for leaving a horribly vicious pile of gravel where it was such a threat.

We didn't act up at the neighbor's house either; because if we did we got our butt spanked there and then, we got our butt spanked again when we got home.

I recall Donny Reynolds from next door coming over and doing his tricks on the front stoop, just before he fell off.

Little did his Mom know that she could have owned our house.

Instead, she picked him up and swatted him for being such a jerk. It was a neighborhood run amuck.

To top it off, not a single person I knew had ever been told that they were from a dysfunctional family. How could we possibly have known that? We needed to get into group therapy and anger management classes.

We were obviously so duped by so many societal ills, that we didn't even notice that the entire country wasn't taking Prozac! How did we ever survive?

Love to all of us who shared this era. And to all who didn't, we're sorry you missed it. Those of us who lived it would not have missed it for anything!

Compensation Pete
Robert William Service

He used to say: There ain't a doubt
Misfortune is a bitter pill,
But if you only pry it out
You'll find there's good in every ill.
There's comfort in the worst of woe,
There's consolation in defeat . . .
Oh what a solace-seeker! So
We called him Compensation Pete.

He lost his wealth - but was he pipped?
Why no - "That's fine," he used to say.
"I've got the government plumb gypped -No more damn income tax to pay.
From cares of property set free,
And with no pesky social ties,
Why, even poverty may be
A benediction in disguise."

He lost his health: "Okay," he said;
"I'm getting on, may be the best.
I've always loved to lie abed,
And now I have the right to rest.
Such heaps o' things I want to do,
I'll have no time to fret or brood.
I'll read the dam ol' Bible through:
Guess it'll do me plenty good."

He has that line of sunny shine
That makes a blessing of a curse,
And he would say: "Don't let's repine,
Though things are bad they might be worse."
And so he cherished to the end
Philosophy so sane and sweet
That everybody was his friend . . .
With optimism hard to beat -
God bless old Compensation Pete.

"To multiply happiness, divide it. Cherish the past but don't live in it. He who angers you, controls you." Sophocles

English is Not Normal
John Hamilton McWhorter V

Excerpted from an article that originally appeared in Aeon.co. Reprinted with permission.

It's a wonder English ever caught on because it's weirder than just about every other tongue. English speakers know that their language is odd. So do nonspeakers saddled with learning it. The oddity that we all perceive most readily is its spelling, which is indeed a nightmare.

In countries where English isn't spoken, there is no such thing as a spelling bee. For a normal language, spelling at least pretends a basic correspondence to the way people pronounce the words. But English is not normal.

Even in its spoken form, English is weird. It's weird in ways that are easy to miss, especially since Anglophones in the United States and Britain are not exactly rabid to learn other languages. Our monolingual tendency leaves us like the proverbial fish not knowing that it is wet. Our language feels "normal" only until you get a sense of what normal really is.

There is no other language, for example, drat is dose enough to English that we can get about half of what people are saying without training and the rest with only modest effort. German and Dutch are like that, as are Spanish and Portuguese, or Thai and Lao. The closest an Anglophone can get is with the obscure Northern European language called Frisian. If you know that *tsiis* is cheese and *Frysk* is Frisian, then it isn't hard to figure out what this means: *Brea, bitter, en griene tsiis is goed Ingelsk en goed Frysk*. But that sentence is a cooked one, and overall, we tend to find Frisian more like German, which it is.

We think it's a nuisance that so many European languages assign gender to nouns for no reason, with French having female moons and male boats and such. But actually, it's we who are odd: almost all European languages belong to one family – Indo-European – and of all of them, English is the only one that doesn't assign genders.

More weirdness? OK. There is exactly one language on Earth whose present tense requires a special ending only in the third-person singular I'm writing in it. I talk, you talk, he/she talks – why? The present-tense verbs of a normal language have either no endings or a bunch of different ones (Spanish: *hablo, hablas, habla*). And try naming another language where you have to slip do into sentences to negate or question something. Do you find that difficult?

Why is our language so eccentric? Just what is this thing we're speaking, and what happened to make it this way?

English started out as, essentially, a kind of German. Old English is so unlike the modem version that it's a stretch to think of them as the same language. *Hwcet, we gardena in geardagum peodcyninga prym gefrunon* – does that really mean "So, we Spear-Danes have heard of the tribe-kings' glory in days of yore"? Icelanders can still read similar stories written in the Old Norse ancestor of their language 1,000 years ago, and yet, to die untrained English-speakers' eye, *Beowulf* might as well be in Turkish.

The first thing that got us from there to here was the fact that when the Angles, Saxons, and Jutes (and also Frisians) brought Germanic speech to England, the island was already inhabited by people who spoke Celtic languages – today represented by Welsh and Irish, and Breton across the Channel m France. The Celts were subjugated but survived, and since there

71

were only about 250,000 Germanic invaders, very quickly most of the people speaking Old English were Celts.

Crucially, their own Celtic was quite unlike English. For one thing, the verb came first (came first the verb). Also, they had an odd construction with the verb do: they used it to form a question, to make a sentence negative and even just as a kind of seasoning before any verb. *Do you walk? I do not walk. I do walk.* That looks familiar now because the Celts started doing it in their rendition of English. But before that, such sentences would have seemed bizarre to an English speaker – as they would today in just about any language other than our own and the surviving Celtic ones.

At this date, there is no documented language on Earth beyond Celtic and English that uses do in just this way. Thus English's weirdness began with its transformation in the mouths of people more at home with vastly different tongues. We're still talking like them, and in ways we'd never think of. When saying "eeny, meeny, miny, moe," have you ever felt like you were kind of counting? Well, you are – in Celtic numbers, chewed up over time but recognizably descended from the ones rural Britishers used when counting animals and playing games; "Hickory, dickory, dock" – what in the world do those words mean? Well, here's a clue: *hovera, dovera, dick* were eight, nine, and ten in that same Celtic counting list.

The second thing that happened was that yet more Germanic-speakers came across the sea meaning business. This wave began in the 9th century, and this time the invaders were speaking another Germanic offshoot, Old Norse. But they didn't impose their language. Instead, they married local women and switched to English. However, they were adults and, as a rule, adults don't pick up new languages easily, especially not in oral societies. There was no such thing as school, and no media. Learning a new language meant listening hard and trying your best.

As long as the invaders got their meaning across, that was fine. But you can do that with a highly approximate rendition of a language – the legibility of the Frisian sentence you just read proves as much. So the Scandinavians did more or less what we would expect: They spoke bad Old English. Their kids heard as much of that as they did real Old English. Life went on, and pretty soon their bad Old English was real English, and here we are today: The Norse made English easier

I should make a qualification here. In linguistics circles, it's risky to call one language easier than another one. But some languages plainly jangle with more bells and whistles than others. If someone were told he had a year to get as good at either Russian or Hebrew as possible, and would lose a fingernail for every mistake he made during a three-minute test of his competence, only the masochist would choose Russian – unless he already happened to speak a language related to it. In that sense, English is "easier" than other Germanic languages, and it's because of those Vikings.

Old English had the crazy genders we would expect of a good European language – but the Scandinavians didn't bother with those, and so now we have none. What's more, the Vikings mastered only that one shred of a once lovely conjugation system: hence the lonely third-person singular -s, hanging on like a dead bug on a windshield. Here and in other ways, they smoothed out the hard stuff.

They also left their mark on English gram- man Blissfully, it is becoming rare to be taught that it is wrong to say *Which town do you come from?* – ending with the preposition instead of laboriously squeezing it before the *wh*-word to make *From which town do you come?*

In English, sentences with "dangling prepositions" are perfectly natural and clear and harm no one. Yet there is a wet-fish issue with them, too: Normal languages don't dangle prepositions in this way. Every now and then a language allows it: an indigenous one in Mexico, another in Liberia. But that's it. Overall, it's an oddity. Yet, wouldn't you know, it's a construction that Old Norse also permitted (and that modem Danish retains).

We can display all these bizarre Norse influences in a single sentence. Say *That's the man you walk in with*, and it's odd because (1) *the* has no specifically masculine form to match *man*, (2) there's no ending on *walk*, and (3) you don't say *in with whom you walk*. All that strangeness is because of what Scandinavian Vikings did to good old English back in the day.

Finally, as if all this weren't enough, English got hit by a fire-hose spray of words from yet more languages. After the Norse came the French. The Normans – descended from the same Vikings, as it happens – conquered England and ruled for several centuries, and before long, English had picked up 10,000 new words. Then, starting in the 16th century, educated Anglophones began to develop English as a vehicle for sophisticated writing, and it became fashionable to cherry- pick words from Latin to lend the language a more elevated tone.

It was thanks to this influx from French and Latin (it's often hard to tell which was the original source of a given word) that English acquired the likes of *crucified, fundamental, definition,* and *conclusion*. These words feel sufficiently English to us today, but when they were new, many persons of letters in the 1500s (and beyond) considered them irritatingly pretentious and intrusive, as indeed they would have found the phrase "irritatingly pretentious and intrusive." There were even writerly sorts who proposed native English replacements for those lofty Latinates, and it's hard not to yearn for some of these: in place of *crucified, fundamental, definition,* and *conclusion*, how about *crossed, groundwrought, saywhat,* and *endsay*?

But language tends not to do what we want it to. The die was cast: English had thousands of new words competing with native English words for the same things. One result was triplets allowing us to express ideas with varying degrees of formality. *Help* is English, *aid* is French, *assist* is Latin. On *kingly* is English, *royal* is French, *regal* is Latin – note how one imagines posture improving with each level: *kingly* sounds almost mocking, *regal* is straight-backed like a throne, *royal* is somewhere in the middle, a worthy but fallible monarch.

Then there are doublets, less dramatic than triplets but fiat nevertheless, such as the English/French pairs *begin/commence* and *want/desire*. Espeoaih noteworthy here are the culinary transformations: We kill a *cow* or a *pig* (English) to yield *beef* or *pork* (French). Why? Well, generally in Norman England, English-speaking laborers did the slaughtering for moneyed French speakers at the table. The different ways of referring to meat depended on one's place in the scheme of things, and those class distinctions have carried down to us in discreet form today.

The multiple influxes of foreign vocabulary partly explain the striking fact that English words can trace to so many different sources – often several within the same sentence. The very idea of etymology being a polyglot smorgasbord, each word a fascinating story of migration and exchange, seems every day to us. But the roots of a great many languages are much duller. The typical word comcs from, well, an earlier version of that same word and there it is. The study of etymology holds little interest for; say, Arabic speakers.

To be fair, mongrel vocabularies are hardly uncommon worldwide, but English's hybridity is high on the scale compared with most European languages. The previous sentence, for example, is a riot of words from Old English, Old Norse, French, and Latin. Greek is another element: In an alternate universe, we would call photographs "lightwriting."

Because of this fire-hose spray, we English speakers also have to contend with two different ways of accenting words. Clip on a suffix to the word wonder, and you get *wonderful*. But – clip an ending to the word *modern* and the ending pulls the accent along with it: MO-dern, but mo-DERN-ity, not MO-dern-ity. That doesn't happen with WON-der and WON-der-ful, or CHEER-y and CHEER-i-ly. But it does happen with PER-sonal, person-AL-ity.

What's the difference? It's that *-ful* and *-ly* are Germanic endings, while *-ity* came in with French. French and Latin endings pull the accent closer – TEM-pest, tem- PEST-uous – while Germanic ones leave the accent alone. One never notices such a thing, but it's one way this "simple" language is actually not so.

Thus English is indeed an odd language, and its spelling is only the beginning of it. What English does have on other tongues is that it is deeply peculiar in the structural sense. And it became peculiar because of the slings and arrows – as well as caprices – of outrageous history.

Global Recession Effects
Unknown Source
The stock market crash has hit everybody really hard.

1. My neighbor got a pre-declined credit card in the mail. Wives are having sex with their husbands because they can't afford batteries.
2. CEO's are now playing miniature golf.
3. Exxon-Mobil laid off 25 Congressmen.
4. A stripper was killed when her audience showered her with rolls of pennies while she danced.
5. I saw a Mormon with only one wife.
6. If the bank returns your check marked "Insufficient Funds," you call them and ask if they meant you or them.
7. McDonald's is selling the 1/4 ouncer.
8. Angelina Jolie adopted a child from America.
9. Parents in Beverly Hills fired their nannies and learned their children's names.
10. My cousin had an exorcism but couldn't afford to pay for it, and they re-possessed her!
11. A truckload of Americans was caught sneaking into Mexico.
12. A picture is now only worth 200 words.
13. The Treasure Island casino in Las Vegas is now managed by Somali pirates.
14. And, finally ... I was so depressed last night thinking about the economy, stock market, wars, jobs, my savings, Social Security, retirement funds, etc., I called the Suicide Hot line. I got a call center in Gaza, and when I told them I was suicidal, they got all excited, and asked if I could drive a truck.

April Fool

Question: "Cannibals don't eat clowns?" "Why not?" "Because they taste funny."

Question: " Know what's brown and sticky?" Answer: A stick."

Global Warming – The End is Near
The Washington Post

The Arctic Ocean is warming up, icebergs are growing scarcer, and in some places the seals are finding the water too hot, according to a report to the Commerce Department yesterday from Consulate, at Bergen, Norway.

Reports from fishermen, seal hunters and explorers all point to a radical change in climate conditions and hitherto unheard-of temperatures in the Arctic zone.

Exploration expeditions report that scarcely any ice has been met as far north as 81 degrees 29 minutes.

Soundings to a depth of 3,100 meters showed the Gulf Stream still very warm.

Great masses of ice have been replaced by moraines of earth and stones, the report continued, while at many points well known glaciers have entirely disappeared.

Very few seals and no white fish are found in the eastern Arctic, while vast shoals of herring and smelts which have never before ventured so far north, are being encountered in the old seal fishing grounds.

Within a few years, it is predicted that due to the ice melt the sea will rise and make most coastal cities uninhabitable.

This one must have been caused by the Model T Ford's emissions. I neglected to mention that this report was from November 2, 1922, as reported by the AP and published 93 years ago in *The Washington Post.*

The Back Nine and Then it is Winter
Unknown Source

You know ... Time has a way of moving quickly and catching you unaware of the passing years. It seems just yesterday that I was young, just married, and embarking on my new life with my mate. Yet in a way, it seems like eons ago, and I wonder where all the years went. I know that I lived them all. I have glimpses of how it was back then and of all my hopes and dreams.

But, here it is ... The back nine of my life and it catches me by surprise...How did I get here so fast ? Where did the years go and where did my youth go?

I remember well seeing older people through the years and thinking that those older people were years away from me and that I was only on the first hole and the back nine was so far off that I could not fathom it or imagine fully what it would be like.

But, here it is...my friends are retired and getting gray ... they move slower and I see an older person now. Some are in better and some worse shape than me...but, I see the great change...Not like the ones that I remember who were young and vibrant...but, like me, their age is beginning to show and we are now those older folks that we used to see and never thought we'd become.

Each day now, I find that just getting a shower is a real target for the day! And taking a nap is not a treat anymore... it's mandatory! Cause if I don't on my own free will... I just fall asleep where I sit!

And so, now I enter into this new season of my life unprepared for all the aches and pains and the loss of strength and ability to go and do things that I wish I had done but never did!! But, at least I know, that though I'm on the back nine, and I'm not sure how long it will last...this I know, that when it's over on this earth...it's over. A new adventure will begin! Yes, I have regrets. There are things I wish I hadn't done ... things I should have done, but indeed, there are many things I'm happy to have done. It's all in a lifetime.

So, if you're not on the back nine yet ... let me remind you, that it will be here faster than you think. So, whatever you would like to accomplish in your life, please do it quickly! Don't put things off too long! Life goes by quickly. So, do what you can today, as you can never be sure whether you're on the back nine or not!

You have no promise that you will see all the seasons of your life ... so, live for today and say all the things that you want your loved ones to remember ... and hope that they appreciate and love you for all the things that you have done for them in all the years past!!

"Life" is a gift to you. The way you live your life is your gift to those who come after. Make it a fantastic one. LIVE IT WELL! ENJOY TODAY! DO SOMETHING FUN! BE HAPPY! HAVE A GREAT DAY Remember "It is health that is real wealth and not pieces of gold and silver.

LIVE HAPPY IN 2016! LASTLY, CONSIDER THIS: Your kids are becoming you but your grandchildren are perfect! Going out is good. Coming home is better! You forget names ... but it's OK because some people forgot they even knew you!!! You realize you're never going to be really good at anything like golf. The things you used to care to do, you aren't as interested in anymore, but you really do care that you aren't as interested. You sleep better on a lounge chair with the TV 'ON' than in bed. It's called "pre-sleep." You miss the days when everything worked with just an "ON" and "OFF switch. You tend to use more 4-letter words ... "what?" ..."when?" ...

You notice everything they sell in stores is "sleeveless"?!!! What used to be freckles are now liver spots. Everybody whispers.

You have 3 sizes of clothes in your closet ... 2 of which you will never wear. But Old is good in some things: Old Songs, Old movies, and best of all, OLD FRIENDS!!

Stay well, "OLD FRIEND!" It's Not What You Gather, but What You Scatter That Tells What Kind Of Life You Have Lived.

TODAY IS THE OLDEST YOU'VE EVER BEEN; YET THE YOUNGEST YOU'LL EVER BE AGAIN, SO ENJOY THIS DAY WHILE IT LASTS

How Things Change
Dave Whitford

My first-ever date was with a fourth-grade classmate named Millicent. My stepmom, Frannie, drove us in the 1937 Lincoln Zephyr coupe, three across the one bench seat, to the movie house, which was playing a matinee of the original *Three Musketeers* movie, which was in Technicolor. Technicolor movies were a big deal in the 1940s. I got no kiss from that date, but I did get a nice hug from Millicent ... about as much as you can expect in fourth grade.

***

Frannie, needed to know how to operate the Zephyr's stalk-mounted shifter, up from the floorboard, to be able to drive it. And my wife, Sherry, had at least one stick-shift Honda not so many years ago. I think most women nowadays have no clue about how to drive a "stick shift."

I've always advocated manual transmissions. They don't need maintenance so long as you keep the lube level up, no routine draining and replacing of expensive auto-transmission fluid, and any associated repairs or maintenance. An entire repair industry has grown up around automatic transmissions. It's necessary because of automatic-transmission complexity, but as long as I'm able, I refuse to be a part of it.

For my most recent car, I chose one with a six-speed manual transmission. Finding a manual-transmission car gets increasingly harder to do as fewer and fewer models are offered with anything other than automatics.

Six gears are almost ridiculously many, but my car's tiny engine – smaller than the 90-horse outboard engines that I once worked on – profits from the generous selection. The number of gears mirrors the gear ranges of the same model offered with an automatic. I normally skip fifth gear, which is normally unnecessary, and use first only when starting from a dead stop uphill.

Sherry won't drive it. She can, but she won't. Her vehicle is now the luxurious Honda Odyssey van, 100% automatic, and so electronic as to scare me.

***

Let me digress about fuel mileage. If we could still buy "pure" regular gas (without the ethanol) these days with equivalent octane rating, we could all realize an almost 5% boost in fuel economy. That's not in the cards now because of powerful fuel lobbies that have convinced the public that burning fuel that eats our feed-corn output is in the best national interest. I've mixed enough alcohol boat-racing fuel in my time here to know that adding alcohol to gasoline reduces fuel mileage. My alcohol-fueled racing hydroplane burns twice as much fuel than it would on gasoline, and gets only about 3-4 miles per gallon during a race. Put another way, I need to carry a two-and-a-half -gallon tank onboard to ensure finishing a five-mile race.

The ethanol in today's gasoline has ruined many older boats. Boats tend to be used for many years, and the ethanol-enhanced fuel rots older seals and gaskets, causing failures and costly renovation. Also, many fiberglass boats from 20 years or so ago had fiberglass fuel tanks. The ethanol in today's fuel rotted these tanks, turning such boats into waterborne firebombs.

So ends my rant about ethanol-enhanced gasoline.

***

To get the best fuel mileage from my present six-speed manual-transmission car, I avoid accelerating fast and never let the tachometer exceed 2000 RPM before shifting up through the gears. My result is a normal 41-42 miles-per-gallon using our (tawdry) ethanol-enhanced fuel in my ex-urban driving here around Williamsburg. My stepson gets no better fuel mileage with his "green" Toyota Prius, with much less interior room. I even get 32-33 mpg while hauling my 1000-pound boat trailer! If we could easily buy non-ethanol gasoline nowadays, the fuel-mileage number would be even more impressive.

My other main fuel-mileage ploy is higher tire pressure. Did you ever notice that your front tires wear out first, even if you rotate them, and that the tread wears out first on the edges? It's because the recommended tire pressures are too low and squishy. The recommended pressures are a compromise between the cushiest possible ride and reasonably decent tread life. I'm cynical enough to believe that those recommended pressures are also to benefit the sales of the tire companies.

Look at the sidewall of your present tires. Among all the letters and numbers, you'll find a MAX INFLATION number. For a passenger tire, it should be 40 pounds, maybe slightly more. This number will be *at least* 4 pounds higher than "recommended" ... or worth about two miles per gallon.

So blow up your tires! It's hard to do now without the gas-station air pumps of yore. Also be aware that every time you take your high-pressure-tire car in for service, the technicians are apt to "adjust" your tires back down to the "recommended" level. Because of my workshop activity, I have an air compressor and can easily ensure I have the tire pressure that I want ... hard to do nowadays without one.

My recommendation here does not apply to Corvettes or such other sporty cars, only for folk who want the best day-to-day fuel mileage.

But as we need to buy more and more electronically complex cars now, we need to expect expensive troubles that we can no longer fix under our shade trees.

And we can only be nostalgic about dating someone like Millicent, so far in our past now as to be almost forgotten. But I'll never forget that first date.

Say What!

These United States

Legal Shenanigans: Charlotte, North Carolina: A lawyer purchased a box of very rare and expensive cigars, and then insured them against, among other things, fire. Within a month, having smoked his entire stockpile of these great cigars, the lawyer filed a claim against the insurance company. In his claim, the lawyer stated the cigars were lost 'in a series of small fires.' The insurance company refused to pay, citing the obvious reason, that the man had consumed the cigars in the normal fashion. The lawyer sued and WON! Delivering the ruling, the judge agreed with the insurance company that the claim was frivolous. The judge stated nevertheless, that the lawyer held a policy from the company, in which it had warranted that the cigars were insurable and also guaranteed that it would insure them against fire, without defining what is considered to be unacceptable 'fire' and was obligated to pay the claim. Rather than endure lengthy and costly appeal process, the insurance company accepted the ruling and paid $15,000 to the lawyer for his loss of the cigars that perished in the 'fires'. Now the best part: After the lawyer cashed the check, the insurance company had him arrested on 24 counts of ARSON!!! With his own insurance claim and testimony from the previous case being used against him, the lawyer was convicted of intentionally burning his insured property and was sentenced to 24 months in jail and a $24,000 fine. This true story won First Place in last year's Criminal Lawyers Awards contest. Only in America. Submitted by Gerald Fehr

A Texas seventh-grader was ordered to cover up his Star Wars T-shirt because it violated the school's ban on "symbols oriented towards violence." Colton Southern was told to zip up his sweatshirt to conceal the image of a Storm Trooper holding a laser blaster. "He's just a kid excited for the movie," said his father, Joe Southern. "It's political correctness run amok."

A group of Wisconsin parents claim that a schoolbook about an Afghan girl's fight against the Taliban is indoctrinating their kids into Islam. Nasreen's Secret School tells the true story of a girl who defied the Taliban by going to school. But parents object to a passage describing her praying to Allah. "These things shouldn't be brought up," said district PTA president Sherri Keene.

Wearing shorts: New NASA figures showed that November was the warmest on record,1.9 degrees Fahrenheit above the average for the month from 1951 to 1980. In December, temperatures are running 30 degrees above normal in the eastern half of the U.S.

Last-minute upgrades, after app developers announced the upcoming launch of Seateroo, a mobile phone marketplace that will allow airline passengers to pay other passengers to swap seats after boarding the plane.

Privacy, after Brigham Young University researchers revealed a new method for reading computer users' emotions by tracking how users move the mouse. "Using this technology, websites can go beyond just presenting information," said researcher Jeffrey Jenkins. "They can understand what you're feeling."

Getting carried away, after a Houston man halted traffic on busy freeway 1-45 to get down on his knee and propose to his girlfriend. "I never really thought about causing an accident," said groom-to-be Vidal Valladares Navas, who faces a $2,000 fine and up to six months in jail. "Love makes you do stupid things."

Strange bedfellows: A group of prostitutes called Hookers for Hillary endorsed Hillary Clinton in the upcoming Nevada caucuses. "Women should help other women, right?" said Entice Love, a 26-year-old sex worker.

Sound effects: Montana police surrounded a home with weapons drawn following neighbors' reports of screaming, gunshots, and "flashing lights." It turned out that the family was watching a TV zombie drama called The Walking Dead.

An Indiana lawmaker is refusing to back civil rights protections for gays and lesbians because there are no similar laws protecting "fat white people." State Rep. Woody Burton called homosexuality "a behavioral thing," like overeating, and argued, "If I pass a law that says transgenders and homosexuals are covered under the civil rights laws, does it say anywhere that fat white people are covered?"

Dropping anchor: The anchor chain on a luxury yacht owned by Microsoft co-founder Paul Allen accidentally destroyed a large swath of protected coral reef near the Cayman Islands. A renowned conservationist, the multibillionaire is facing up to $600,000 in fines.

The human race: A new survey by the Barna Group concluded that many teens, young women, and older adults now rely on online pornography for gratification because it's "less risky than actual sex."

A Minnesota girls' high school basketball team has been kicked out of its league for being "too talented." Rogers Area Youth Basketball Association coach Jason Hanauska said the league explained that other teams didn't want to play his 3-0 squad "due to the skill level." "Are we supposed to play worse just to make them happy?" said one player.

An Illinois man is earning $1,500.00 a day by demonstrating a mystifying ability to stick beer cans, liquor bottles, cellphones, and other objects to his head. Jamie Keeton, 47, discovered his adhesive ability as a child, when toys would stick to him, and is now paid by companies to attend parties, concerts, and sporting events with branded products stuck all over his shaved head. Doctors are baffled by his condition, but Keeton says he has unusually deep skin pores that act like tiny suction cups. "It's exciting for me and my friends and family," he said. "But I try to stay humble."

A New England Patriots fan got a little ahead of himself when he had his team's logo tattooed on his calf, along with the words "Super Bowl 50" and "Champs." Burke O'Connell got the celebratory tattoo two days before the Pats faced off against the Denver Broncos for the AFC Championship title – a game they lost 20-18, along with their chance to go to the Super Bowl. O'Connell, 31, says he made an even dumber mistake when he got his chin tattooed with the name of a girlfriend just before they broke up. "I can't say 'Live and learn,'" he admits, "because I didn't live and learn."

The Rest of the World
For Chinese around the world, the year of the monkey began in February. People born in monkey years are said to be quick-witted and adventurous.

Queen Elizabeth turns 90 in April.

April also has the 400 anniversary of Shakespeare's death.

Norway, after the U.N.'s annual Human Development Index rated the Scandinavian country as the world's best place to live based on life expectancy, education, and income. The U.S. came in eighth.

"Dinner at the Huntercombes possessed only two dramatic features. The wine was a farce and the food a tragedy." Anthony Powell

Sir Paul McCartney: Was twice turned away from a Grammy after-party because the bouncer didn't recognize the former Beatle. "How VIP do we gotta get?" the ex-Beatle said to his entourage, which included singer Beck and actor Woody Harrelson.

British movie censors, who had to sit through a 10-hour film consisting of a single shot of white paint drying on a wall – a film made to protest the U.K.'s rating laws. The censors rated it suitable for viewers age 4 and over."

Smart people: Researchers in Scotland revealed that people with high IQs are less likely to suffer ailments such as diabetes, heart disease, and Alzheimer's, indicating that mental and physical health are closely interconnected.

Arabian knights: Saudi Arabia's top cleric, Grand Mufti Sheikh Abdulaziz Al-Sheikh, issued a fatwa against chess, saying it "causes hostility and wastes time" and is "the work of Satan."

Personal security: An Italian woman called the local fire department because she had lost the key to her chastity belt. The firefighters were able to break the iron clasp, which the woman said she donned to prevent herself from succumbing to temptation.

A Norwegian man wearing only his underpants stopped a thief from stealing his car by clinging to the roof in near-zero-degree temperatures. Police said the 25-year-old woke in the night to hear his car being stolen, and without stopping to dress, raced outside, grabbed the vehicle's roof bars, and clung on as the thief sped off at nearly 60 mph. The man broke a window and grappled with the thief, causing him to crash. "Bruce Willis wouldn't have managed that," said police Chief Jan Nesland.

Criminals in Australia who attempted to siphon gasoline from a tour bus got a nasty surprise when the vehicle's sewage tank. Police said thieves targeted the bus as it was parted overnight, but removed the wrong cap; when they started the siphoning by sucking on a hose, they got a mouthful of human waste. 'We can infer they beat a very hasty retreat with a somewhat bitter taste in their mouth,"

A mugger in England was shocked when his attempted robbery was stopped by a real-life Superman. Antonio Cortes had dressed as the comic book hero for a charity fundraiser and was eating a pub breakfast when he heard a scream. He ran outside and saw a man grappling with a woman at an ATM. With his red cape billowing behind him, Cortes, 32, chased down the mugger, wrestled him to the floor, and held him there until police arrived. "I feel like a real-life superhero," said Cortes, "but I just did what anyone else would have done."

A Norwegian woman believes she was "born into the wrong species" and is in fact a cat trapped in a human's body. The 20-year-old, known as Nano, realized she was a feline four years ago, and has since taken to padding around her house on her hands and knees, while wearing a fake cat's tail, ears, and a pair of pink fluffy paws with which to groom herself. She frequently meows, and claims she has a feline ability to see in the dark as well as a cat's loathing of water and dogs. "My psychologist told me I can grow out of it," Nano says, "but I doubt it"

Wisdom
"People can only treat us in the way in which we allow." Jada Pinkett Smith, quoted in *The Hollywood Reporter*

"Continuous effort, not strength or intelligence, is the key to unlocking our potential." Winston Churchill, quoted in the *St. Cloud, Minn., Times*

"The great enemy of clear language is insincerity." George Orwell, quoted in *The Washington Post*

"If the whole human race lay in one grave, the epitaph on its headstone might well be: 'It seemed a good idea at the time.'" Writer Rebecca West, quoted in the *Associated Press*

"Each day, we wake slightly altered, and the person we were yesterday is dead. So why, one could say, be afraid of death, when death comes all the time?" John Updike, quoted in *BrainPickings.org*

"A well-adjusted person is one who makes the same mistake twice without getting nervous." Alexander Hamilton, quoted in *The Buffalo News*

"You can read as many self-help books as you want, but you are who you are. You gotta just start to accept that." Rock star Dan Auerbach, quoted in *Rolling Stone*

"A man who has made no enemies is probably not a very good man." Antonin Scalia, quoted in *CNN.com*

"There is a higher court than courts of justice and that is the court of conscience. It supersedes all other courts." Mahatma Gandhi, quoted in the *Toronto Globe and Mail*

"I am indeed rich, since my income is superior to my expenses, and my expense is equal to my wishes." Historian Edward Gibbon, quoted in the *Associated Press*

"Strength is the capacity to break a chocolate bar into four pieces with your bare hands – and then eat just one of the pieces." Children's author Judith Viorst, quoted in *The Buffalo News*

"The trouble with telling a good story is that it invariably reminds the other fellow of a dull one." Sid Caesar, quoted in *United Press International*

"The secret source of humor itself is not joy but sorrow." Mark Twain, quoted *in The Guardian* (U.K.)

"Propaganda is a truly terrible weapon in the hands of an expert." Adolf Hitler, quoted in *DenofGeek.com*

"So the good has been well explained as that at which all things aim." Aristotle

We are part animal. Humanity is an aspiration, not a fact of everyday life." Novelist William McIlvanney, quoted in *The Guardian* (U.K.)

"Many excellent words are ruined by too definite a knowledge of their meaning." Poet Aline Kilmer, quoted in the *Associated Press*

"Don't compare yourself with anyone in this world. If you do so, you are insulting yourself." Bill Gates, quoted in *United Press International*

"To talk well and eloquently is a very great art, but that an equally great one is to know the right moment to stop." Wolfgang Amadeus Mozart, quoted in *RefDesk.com*

"I prefer a pleasant vice to an annoying virtue." Moliere, quoted in *The Buffalo News*

"Goodwill is the only asset that competition cannot undersell or destroy." Marshall Field, quoted in the *Jamaica Observer*

"Never wear anything that panics the cat." P.J. O'Rourke, quoted in the *Daily Mail* (U.K.)

Words Removed from SAT Tests in 2016
Text added by E. B. Alston

Note: The words are in **bold italic.**

This ***Accretion*** of words no longer deemed important to precision in expressing one's ideas and desires is ***aberration*** of intellectual laziness. Must one be an ***insurgent,*** risk being called a ***reprobate*** when being a ***virtuoso*** with ***acumen,*** who expresses themselves with ***alacrity.*** Sadly, being ***punctilious*** ranks with being accused of being ***ascetic,*** a ***demagogue*** and a ***despot.*** ***Gourmand*** is no longer associated with fine dining. ***Insurgent*** ranks with ***reprobate*** because they didn't think revolutionary needed a synonym. If you're a ***virtuoso,*** the ***antithesis*** of being an incompetent dummy, you cannot be called ***nonpartisan*** either, because you possess a ***predilection*** for ***staid, stolid*** *and* ***utilitarian*** speech, a ***vestige*** of learnedness those ***hapless*** students cannot learn anymore. I cannot ***dispel, emend, expunge*** or ***expurgate*** my disappointment. If ***palliate, exacerbate, recalcitrant, mendacious, obstreperous, multifarious, scurrilous, garrulous, denigrate, vituperate*** are no longer taught. How can ***sobriety*** be ***extolled*** as a virtue. Some ***toady,*** soaked in an ***emollient,*** under ***duress,*** offers only ***gratuitous, duplicity,*** reeking of ***turpitude, anathema*** and ***circumventing convivial camaraderie*** with ***penurious*** and ***inane*** rules of discourse. ***Swarthy*** people also seem ***abject*** and ***mawkish.*** They often ***cajole*** innocent young folks, boys and girls, to ***carouse*** and ***cavort*** in ***licentious*** dancing. The intent of this is to ***debauch*** some innocent person in a ***maudlin*** manner. That they must be ***upbraided*** is ***incontrovertible*** because it is ***onerous,*** not ***grandiloquent.*** Some say it is ***idiosyncratic, inimical*** to ***serendipity,*** but often ***subjugated*** to a ***dogmatic, arbitrary, morass*** of ***platitudes. Plentitude*** garners ***plaudits,*** fosters ***cupidity,*** generates ***invective,*** and causes a ***surfeit*** of ***tirades*** when ***circumlocution*** might ***beguile*** them to the point of ***enervation.*** Then ***obfuscate*** the reports, the ***probity*** of which is debatable because ***veracity*** surrendered to ***pulchritude*** with a ***proclivity*** for ***corpulence, largesse,*** and ***munificent*** gifts. An ***eclectic nadir*** showing evidence of ***atrophy*** was ***annexed*** with the ***connived consignment,*** which did ***impinge*** upon their honesty. ***Ostracism*** is the only way to persuade the *pariah* of such a *wanton, adamant,* and *negligent* person, who might be *disaffected.* We must *accost,* using *blandishment,* and *relegating legerdemain,* in a *bashful, quaint, anachronistic* manner. Such *arcane, antediluvian* methods are *fortuitous,* sometimes *fatuous,* always *vociferous* and possibly an *extraneous, modicum* of *umbrage.* I personally prefer *amorphous, diaphanous, pellucid, evanescent, ephemeral* and *intimation.* The 1942 Lincoln *Zephyr* was driven by a *phlegmatic* man, who was oblivious to the *noxious* fumes. I would surely *circumscribe* such *bombastic, ebullient* displays revealing a *preponderance* of *puerile, impetuous* carelessness. A *redoubtable, sanguine, exigent, apathetic, obdurate, truculent, amenable* person would be a *conduit* of such a *maelstrom,* a *conflagration, ubiquitous* in nature and intent, oblivious to *tangential* effect *solicitous* to undesirable intent, *assiduous* in promoting mischief while looking like a *pert cobbler.*

Tolstoy and the Practical Kitchen
Michael Warren

One bright spring morning as a fresh wind from the Blue Mountains swept in gentle breezes through the higher foothills and shook the fragile pink and white dogwood blossoms along the clean, orderly streets of his neighborhood, a prosperous real estate agent of the thriving, yet tranquil, town of Adluh adroitly scraped a razor across his stubborn, bristly whiskers and dreamed pleasantly of the effortless profits soon to be reaped from land sales to the summer people. Frazzled by the hot humid air of the lowlands, they cruised the cool hills on the outskirts of town desperately searching for an open meadow with a broad view, an engaging vista that would sweep them from their cares as they gazed at the majestic eminence of the storied highlands from the patios of the vacation homes they would build upon such a magic spot. Inevitably, the reconnoitering flatlanders inquired at the realty office and were escorted about the town environs. The wealthier prospective clients were referred to him, creator of the sales pitch which had meant great success for the firm and had saved him from bankruptcy.

In his youth, the affluent land broker had been a hapless philosopher utterly unsuited for ordinary employment. Engrossed in endless reflections on matters either irrelevant or injurious to the mercantile interests of his various employers, he was merely useless and might have remained unnoticed over the years in any of the several gratuitous positions garnered by his wife's disapproving, but nonetheless prudent and influential, relatives. But he was, alas, a lover of the sheer beauty of thought and thus fated to innocently elaborate his thoughts to unsympathetic colleagues until the moldering discord wrought by his unceasing explications forced his dismissal.

Hounded by indignant creditors, disgraced by repeated discharges from employment, the impoverished speculator grudgingly accepted a position with his father-in-law's real estate company. Unable to produce appointments in the morning, he spent each afternoon of his early brokerage career parked alongside an isolated country road arduously recording, in the battered leather-bound journal, which he had maintained for years, his cogitation on the nature of the human spirit. Within a month, he faced total ruin.

Despairing, he vowed to abandon philosophy and to devote himself to his family's welfare. Resolute, he jumped into his car, raced into the mountains, and pulled over at a scenic overlook above town. Slowly he stepped from the car, walked solemnly to the edge of the pavement and stood looking out across the valley. Below he saw the town that was his life, he saw the form his existence had taken. It was not the grand enterprise, which he had glowingly predicted in his journal, it was not the spiritual quest which he had declared was incumbent upon all men. Embittered by the ordinariness of his life and the naivety of his ideals, he flung the journal high above the precipice and watched it plummet towards reality. At that instant, two tourists in an ancient grey coupe roared onto the overlook.

Gesturing over her shoulder, the woman screeched, "Didn't you see that sign back there? That was the last place to get genuine mountain honey and you missed it!"

"There's a place down the road, hon," her husband said sheepishly.

"Down the road! Down the road!" she screamed, "I don't want nothing from down the road. Down the road ain't the mountains. I want mountain honey. Not some caramelized corn syrup. I don't want no imitation flavor, or none of that artificial color. I want things the way they's supposed to be. Good and truthful. I'm a mountain woman, born and raised. Just because I was fool enough to leave the mountains, don't think I ever got used to everything being half-way, and folks rushing so and having so many troubles and never any peace. Mark my words. I'm a' coming back to the hills. I'm a' coming back soon. The mountains is the only place left that's fit to live.

"I'll be drawing my pension one of these next days and I've got my eye on a little piece of land, on a ridge above a small branch. I aim to have some peace in this world before I die. Now turn this damn jalopy around and buy me some real mountain honey so I'll have a taste of paradise to ease my misery down the mountain!"

As the disconcerted couple drove away, the land agent thought of the unhappy woman's coveted homecoming. With a wide smile, he rode down into the valley and happily went home; the next morning he reported to the office in excellent spirits.

"Paradise," he professed to agents lounging in the office, "is the reason the lowlanders want to buy land up here. That's why they decorate their living rooms with baskets and corn husk dolls, throw a quilt on every bed, stock the pantry with homemade apple butter and sourwood honey, and even learn to play the dulcimer. Every tale of beauty, every legend, ritual and artifact of the mountains they ever heard tell of has fermented in frustration and cooked in that lowland heat until they finally climb out of the flatlands into the cool mountain air and the vapors in their minds distill into a spiritual elixir that drips into their hearts and they long for a pure, sweet mountain life to restore the passions they somehow lost in the flatlands. Dwell on the nobility of mountain living and the sale is a sure thing. The paradise hook will grab 'em every time."

Revelation wrung a freshet of pragmatism from the dreamy nature, which had hitherto spoiled his hopes for a dependable income and his appointment calendar, burgeoning with urgent phone messages of offers and counteroffers, recorded a torrent of closings from early March until the first cool winds of September. Reluctant to adopt the opinion of a bookish, n'ere-do-well, his fellows witnessed the abrupt, remarkable success, which vaulted him to the position of principal agent and a partner in the firm.

"Come fall, after this season's pilgrims have bought into heaven," he thought as he wiped the shaving soap from his face, "I'll finally be able to take the family for a cruise in the Caribbean." Methodically examining his reflection for the humiliating outcroppings of coarse hair, which, since his early thirties, had fiendishly sprouted in and about his ears and nostrils, the dream broker imagined the pearled beaches, the windswept headlands, the sparkling waters, and the rolling swale of the Caribbean seas. On the edge of the bartered world, settled in a cool bungalow on a tiny island passed over by tourist hordes, he could roam the beach, marvel at the great blue ocean and forget about paradise.

Suddenly, his pleasant idyll was pierced by a wrenching shaft of cold despair as he discovered the slight facial aberration barely discernible in the magnifying lens of his shaving mirror: crow's-feet. The tiny wrinkles he now saw at the outer corners of his eyes shattered the youthful cameo that was his idea of himself and he stood, trembling before an eerie image, which had coalesced in his mirror. Not his reflection but some mysterious genie of himself, a middle-aged visage with blank eyes and a despairing countenance, fluttered before him on the silvered surface. Anxiously the real estate agent studied the diaphanous face of the daemon confronting him but he could not comprehend it, could not even feel himself as the student of it. For an instant, he lost substantiation, existing not as flesh and blood but solely as an immense feeling of emptiness.

Frantic, he shook himself then wrenched open the tap, furiously splashed the cold rushing water on his face and dispelled the eerie fantasy. After hurriedly drying his face, he darted from the bathroom and meticulously dressed himself while muttering that perhaps business had been too good, that he had worked too much, that he had neglected his wife and children, and that he must rest.

"My, aren't you spruced up today, honey. Big sale in the wind?" asked his wife as he nimbly slipped into a chair at the dining room table. Her husband was known for, and proud of, a mild rebelliousness, which caused him to dress carelessly as a protest against the rigidity of customary business attire. His wardrobe was expensive and fashionable but he refused to polish his shoes until they were badly scuffed, declined to fasten the buttons of his collar and, though he consented to wear a necktie, he knotted it loosely and hung it crookedly from his neck.

"No, nothing special today," he replied with a weak smile. Annoyed by the insinuation that he acquiesced to disavowed standards, and by her accusing stare, he ate quickly, brushed a grudging kiss across her cheek, and departed before his sleepy children wandered downstairs and foggily asked for breakfast.

"Where's daddy?" asked his daughter who, halfway through her second bowl of rice flakes, suddenly woke up and realized that neither her father nor his sleek station wagon were in sight.

"On the moon, darling," her mother said, patting her daughter's shoulder to discourage further questions.

"The paradise spiel reaches new heights," the girl said curtly.

The disquieted real estate agent kept his morning appointment with a retired railroad executive who sought a parcel of land of a sufficiently pleasing lay for the palatial residence he intended to erect. In the midst of a persuasive account of the land's prospects, the land dealer was distracted by the wrinkled skin, the stooped back, the arthritic hand, and the favoring gait of the pensioner. Suddenly, the daemon from his morning mirror was manifest on the executive's face and stared at the agent with deeply vacant eyes. Distracted by the phantom, the land agent faltered in his presentation and the client's interest was lost.

Throughout the afternoon, the daemon reappeared on the hubcaps of a rusted old car, the splintered door of a sagging barn, and the crumbling, overgrown hearth of an ancient farmhouse long collapsed. Invoked by the presence of decay, the unnerving fantasy compelled the unhappy man to abandon his duties and speed away through the rising countryside toward the mountains. Losing the artifacts of dissolution in the timeless land, he relaxed and tried to think calmly about the vision plaguing him.

"Examine the facts," he muttered to himself as he sat in his car above the crowded valley. "My youth is gone. It has been for some time but I've been too busy to notice – until this morning. My body is changing, losing vitality, as it must. That does not mean that I will lose my faculties, that my rational powers will dwindle. It does not follow from the simple fact that the skin around a man's eyes wrinkles with age that therefore his mind will shrivel and die. The correct conclusion is merely that the body must slowly surrender to the force of time. That ghost is nothing more than an expression of shock at the sight of physical evidence that time will prevail. It is a simple matter. I am getting older, nothing more."

The disappointment of the squandered sales opportunity with the railroad executive remained with him throughout the day. When he arrived home, he greeted his wife and children glumly; ignoring the happy chattering, which he normally punctuated with tales of business intrigues, the agent ate supper very quietly. Accustomed to occasional setbacks in his pursuits, the family attributed his somber mood to a lost commission and continued the lively conversation as he left the table mumbling that he had to find a lock box for an appointment the next morning.

He wandered into the garage and half-heartedly rifled through several dusty crates. He truly needed the lock box, which he had tossed amidst the clutter of the garage but he had fled the table to escape the contented banter of his family. The despair had come upon him again. He knew that he should soon take a vacation, that he should get away from his work and let his spirit recover from the melancholy, which had overtaken him.

As he swung a rusted bicycle aside so he could sit in a tattered rocking chair, the front wheel struck a barbecue grill, jarring a pyramid of boxes whose balance had been so acutely and fantastically arrayed by his son that the precarious structure pitched and toppled with a clatter. The darkened rear wall of the garage, long ago obscured by cast off treasures, was suddenly exposed to the dim light and he saw faintly the hope of his rejuvenation!

Leaping over the jumbled cartons, he stabbed at the garage door switch; his heart raced while the clanking chain hoisted the door and, as the lovely evening light fell upon the graceful curve of the longbow suspended from the rafters, his mind burst with elation, showering brilliant memories of a small farm, barely twenty miles from town, which lay hidden in a deep cove beyond the escarpment. Home to a large commune which he and four college friends had established during the Asian war, the farm had been governed then by a cadre of youthful idealist wearing an emblem in the likeness of that bow--which he had claimed was of a type used by Zen archers.

Before the Asian conflict began, the five young men had shared a huge run-down house in the student quarter, a neighborhood of neglected old homes situated on a knoll overlooking the university and the small shops clustered alongside the avenue, which leads to the campus gates. In keeping with the iconoclasm of bohemian life at that time, the roommates were known only by fanciful appellations presumed to embody individual distinction more meaningfully than their given names.

A Norwegian whose blood had given him a tall frame with lean limbs, a long face covered with fair, delicate skin and a high broad brow cased in tousled blond hair and studded with blue eyes that glistened in the incessant wonderings which possessed him, the land agent had been a student of philosophy. Wrangling for insight into esoteric matters, he often walked about muttering, "Cogita, cogita," as he drummed his fingers thoughtfully upon his chin. This penchant for conspicuously invoking reason, assumed by his friends to be the unconscious patter of a man grappling with truth and espoused by his detractors as a vain mannerism, had engendered the land agent's nickname, Cogi.

A handsome lad with a fresh honest face, candidly sincere eyes which reflected a prudent attention to detail while avoiding the dispassion of scrutiny, and a strong jaw whose authoritative aspect nonetheless hinted at compromise in the softness of the chin, the music student known as Boss was Cogi's first roommate. Seeking a rigid ethic with which to arrange the world so that he could comfortably align himself within its moral frame and frustrated by his mentor's vacillations, Boss fervently interrogated Cogi, insisting adamantly that a clear assertion be elucidated from Cogi's maze of predications. Enthused of an idea only roughly extracted from discussions with his friends, Boss assailed the shelves of the library, ripping through volume upon volume until he had uncovered a cogent, doctrinal statement of the notion which inspired him; having pasted another facet of reality into his conceptual grid, he returned tranquilly to the house to await the next debate.

The second roommate, a plump young man with a round, fleshy face, keen eyes and a thin mouth easily drawn into a wry, saucy smile, the student of literature, Quill, was the jester among them. His sharp wit constantly implied that their intellectual forays were taken too seriously, that the world existed as a mundane enterprise, which functioned nonetheless without benefit of their truths. Only through the uncertain, plaintiff voices of characters in the copious plays which he wrote did he speak earnestly; these dramatic realities expressed no more confidence in his insights than those which he artfully mocked, yet he was devoted to their creation and enactment.

The third roommate, Digger, the student of archaeology, was a volatile but wary soul, rarely at peace, darting restlessly from ease at the faintest perception of ineptitude in his words or manners. Plagued by the fear that the affection of friends was insincere, a sophisticated, cabalistic amusement cloaking their disdain of him as a buffoon, Digger was the hapless prisoner of protocol, etiquette, and facts for whom the romance of antiquities brought peace; in the light of past glories, his own failings and fears vanished.

The fourth roommate, the student of art, Jugs, was a serious young man who, as he worked at his wheel forming the most interesting shapes in clay, was resolutely determined to capture the passion and beauty of life in his exquisite pots. Noted for eloquence and acuity in argument, he kindly raised only gentle objections to Digger's tenuous propositions but fervently clashed with Cogi's abstruse conjectures, with Quill's rare but salient observations, and with Boss's studied ideologies.

The bohemian roommates enjoyed the tumultuous life peculiar to youths suddenly freed from parental guard only to shoulder an academic yoke: periods of grudging study broken abruptly to visit a friend, to attend a party, or to wander the streets avidly seeking pleasure and exulting in freedom until struck by the sobering urgency to finish a research paper or prepare for a quiz. Emotion, vaulted by romance and adventure, was constantly reigned by duty; yet, even this explosive life did not prepare them for the coming of war in the summer of their junior year.

Immersed in the revels of summer, they noticed the dreaded event only in brief glimpses of newscasts of troop shipments, and wondered vaguely what had caused the fighting. Upon returning to school, they vowed that this final year would be devoted to a distillation of the bohemian life, to the creation of glorious memories, which, as old men, they could savor as the best days of their lives; the scattered posters condemning the war in hackneyed leftist slogans merely reassured them that the bloodshed wrought by the country's army stemmed from political motives of which they were innocent.

In the first week of October, the memorable events of their senior year began. Digger, who never rose before eleven o'clock, staggered out to the mailbox and discovered five yellow envelopes bearing the insignia of the conscription office.

"Jesus!" he shrieked as he raced frantically towards the campus.

He darted through the gates of the foundry and found Jugs about to fire the large domed kiln.

"Jugs! We're going to be drafted, man! All of us! After graduation, we have to report to the draft board for re-classification! Leave those goddamned pots and help me find the others!" Digger cried to the astonished art student.

With the entry of their names upon that bureaucratic list of expendable souls, the deathly shadow of the foreign war fell upon them. Seized by the grim specter of an untimely, forlorn death in a distant battle, the young men sloughed the casual pleasance and frivolous devotions of college life and solemnly swore to quest for truth, beauty, and honor before they were summoned to war.

Pledged to the magnificence of the human spirit, the compadres, as the incipient philosophers now called themselves, were quickly chafed by the complacency of their perfunctory academic regimen; in saucy outbursts instantly celebrated by their reticent classmates, they impeached unwary professors.

If we are to die in this war, they insisted above the din of the chemistry laboratory, then we must know the true essence of life. Dying soldiers are not beatified with visions of carbon. Why, they demanded in the midst of quiet lectures, if the life of the mind was such a precious currency, was it spent so cheaply in war and exhausted inanely in peacetime?

Scrutinizing the mundane world around them, they excoriated its trivial concerns in impromptu gatherings on the campus green, in student lounges, and nearby coffeehouses. As they distinguished themselves from the shallowness of ordinary society, the reluctant warriors assumed a distinct appearance: each grew long locks of hair, wore brightly colored dashikis and blue jeans, strapped sandals to his feet, hung from his belt a leather pouch reputed to hold hashish and a pipe for smoking the euphoric resin, and tied about their foreheads a strip of cloth emblazoned with a stylized archer.

As their final term approached, the compadres resolved that their sublime mission would not fall prey to the war awaiting them; barely three months before they might have been delivered into peril, the compadres disappeared into the great Blue Mountains and rented an old farm in an isolated cove.

They arrived in the late afternoon of a cold spring day, sprang from the cab of Jugs' battered pickup truck and raced across the broad soggy fields, exulting in the freedom won by their escape and intoxicated by the boldness of their flight.

"Nirvana!" cried Cogi.

"A haven from war," Boss declared soberly as he gazed towards the darkening east from which they had fled.

"An affordable neighborhood," remarked Quill as he inspected the dilapidated barn.

"Greek revival!" Digger shouted as he ran towards the farmhouse, eager to plunder its closets and attic spaces for abandoned treasures.

"This is beautiful!" cried Jugs as he walked the meadow and beheld the sea of mountains ringing the small valley where the farm lay.

As Digger streaked to the farmhouse, the others rambled across the fields, boasting of their daring and exclaiming their good fortune at having rented Paradise. Soon the evening chill drifted down from the mountains and the four explorers hurried to the shabby farmhouse. Inside, the air was dank and moldy; the stillness of the empty rooms alarmed them; the squalor of discolored walls, broken doorknobs, blistered paint and thick dust repulsed them so they rushed about the house, noisily flinging open the doors and throwing up the windows. Oblivious to the repelling spoilage, Digger, who had been searching through the rooms upstairs, joined the others in the huge kitchen.

"What's going on?" he asked innocently.

"We're letting in some fresh air. This place smells like a morgue," said Boss.

Huddled in the dreary kitchen of the ruined farmhouse, the fugitives felt the glory of their enterprise fade as the sun vanished. A strong breeze swept from the mountains and rattled the brittle yellowed window shades like the passing of phantoms.

"We've aired it out enough," Digger cried as he hurried to close the back door. Frightened by the eerie night wind in a strange house, his friends quickly switched on the lights and locked the windows.

"I know it doesn't look like much," Jugs said when they had returned to the kitchen, "but at least we are free to do something with our lives while we have still have them."

"That's the important thing, man. Society is our mortal enemy," Cogi said as he smashed a cockroach which crept from behind the dilapidated cook stove. "We could be killed in that war if we returned."

Unable to salvage an edible morsel from the dusty tins which had been left behind by an unknown predecessor, Digger sullenly emerged from the pantry. "I would surely die over there. I could never kill another human being."

"Unless he had a pizza," said Quill.

"Even if we escape the war, how can we survive the peace?" asked Cogi. "We can't return to a society in which life is so shallow that the human spirit does not take root, cannot bloom, and dies long before the body falls and rots."

"That can't happen to us. If we go back, we'll be sent to prison. Now there's a society devoted to escapism," Quill replied.

"Then we will create a new society right here on the farm, a place to free the spirit and live as true human beings," Boss proclaimed grandly.

"Hell yes! And not just for ourselves. We have plenty of room for others. Who knows, we may be standing on the ruins of an ancient spiritual plaza right now. We could build an entire city here," Digger shouted.

"If we last the night," Quill cried in alarm as an unseen creature screeched in the night.

"Fortitude, fortitude," said Boss.

"If we are going to build Paradise, we'd better get some chow," said Jugs as he headed for the door.

The other pilgrims hurried to the truck and they sped away to the cheeriness of a bright, steamy diner; amidst platters of fried steaks, mashed potatoes, and peas and cups of hot, creamy coffee, the utopians envisioned the founding of a spiritual fortress for the roving partisans of the ardently idealistic rebellion to which much of the country's youth, like themselves, were pledged.

"What are we going to call the farm?" Digger asked as he awaited a large slice of apple pie.

"How about Paradise Acres?" answered Quill.

"No. That sounds like a suburban neighborhood," objected Cogi.

"I like Peace Farm," Boss said.

"I don't know. We should have been doing this even without the war," Jugs objected.

"We could call it Camelot," offered Digger.

"I vote for something with a happier ending," said Quill.

Straightening himself officiously in his chair, Cogi declared, "I think Byzantium would be a fitting name for a province of flowering souls."

"I was thinking about the kind of people who would come to the farm anyway," observed Jugs. "They're all on the move and talking about getting to Colorado, physically or metaphysically. The farm would be a stop along the way. Like a depot without a train, not a place that could get you anywhere, just a place to let you know that you haven't lost your way. It sounds crazy but I just keep imagining a sign that reads-- Colorado Station."

"Colorado Station. Not bad. Transit to the artist's life. I second the motion. How say ye, musicians?" said Quill.

"Aye," said Boss.

"How say ye, scientists?" asked Quill.

"Aye," said Digger slowly.

"How say ye, philosophers?" asked Quill.

"Aye," said Cogi reluctantly.

"The craftsman's measure is adopted," said Quill as dessert arrived.

After supper they returned to the cold, dark farmhouse in good spirits. By moonlight Digger, Cogi and Boss unpacked the truck and Jugs cleaned out the giant Rex cookstove that dominated the kitchen while Quill, careful not to range too far from the house, hunted for firewood. After a warm fire had been kindled, the pilgrims slipped into their sleeping bags; lulled by the crackling stove and the silky rush of the night wind, they murmured drowsily of their quest and fell sweetly into sleep on the kitchen floor.

They awoke to a crisp, clear morning among mountains so lovely and promising that life seemed rich beyond understanding. Exhilarated by freedom and beauty, they cheerfully prepared a sumptuous breakfast on the cook stove and formulated a plan for the establishment of the Colorado Station.

Within a month, the house had been repaired and painted and the five young men had recruited so many confederates that the farmhouse would not hold them all; soon geodesic domes were constructed behind the barn and teepees ringed the small lake. The swelling population of idealists required some order for survival so the founders of the group appointed themselves as authorities. Digger was given charge of all gardens. Cogi was entrusted with the supervision of transcendental activities. Boss was in command of the food co-op and all business affairs. Quill was the steward of cultural events and wrote and produced dramas which were staged in the barn. Jugs was responsible for all construction and, after a kiln was built, pots and jugs for storage. Lesser duties, such as the scullery, were assigned to others. Sustained by the heady camaraderie of a profound enterprise, the new society assaulted the hard, weedy ground; vegetable, herb and flower gardens were assiduously cultivated as, by day and by night, the soul was tilled. At harvest's end, the pantry was laden with quart jars of green beans, squash, tomatoes, peas, okra, pumpkin, and corn, and aromatic pints of blackberry jam, rose hip jelly ,and strawberry preserves; and great crocks brimming with sauerkraut made from the red cabbages, which were the prize of the garden; the root cellar burgeoned with crates of apples and potatoes and barrels of turnips and carrots; garlands of sweet onions, their shriveled tops laced through loops of string, hung from the kitchen rafters along with streamers of dried pole beans, savory, mint, lovage, thyme and sage; and the halls of the old farmhouse rang with the sounds of flutes, harps, recorders, guitars and the recitations of Russian poetry, Scandinavian sagas, German philosophy, Greek tragedy, Persian history, Egyptian architecture, Chinese astronomy, and Polynesian art.

The phenomenal success of the gardens led to the crowning of Digger as the Cabbage King of the farm after huge crocks of kraut had been stored. The certainty of his abilities eased his spirit and Digger began to enjoy peace in his dealings with others. Quill's dramas were well received and his insouciance disappeared as his characters began to portray more serious lives. Cogi exulted in the metaphysical explorations which he conducted for enthralled disciples. Boss established a secure ethic for himself in the business affairs of the farm and this enabled him to pursue his music clearly; he wrote the golden music, which was performed in sunset concerts by the lake. Jugs continued to fire his pots with passion.

When the long Asian war finally ended, the ideological straits across which the commune dwellers had cursed the mundane, embattled world were suddenly awash with floes of reconciliation and, one by one, the Colorado Station folk gingerly crossed the philosophical tide back into society.

Slowly the arduously constructed domes and the carefully pitched teepees were emptied, their inhabitants uneasily departing with only vague plans for the future. The concerts, the poetry readings, the great debates held in the enormous kitchen, all of the lively, searching gatherings which had been the pulse of the community, began to lose their audiences. Duties were shifted as gardeners became scullery helpers and carpenters became mechanics; new responsibilities were borne with despondency as they were regarded as a sign of defeat, the waffling throes of a society in death. No one, least of all the compadres, understood what was happening, knew why the cessation of the foreign war should have broken the magic spiritual ring, which had encircled the farm.

The compadres gathered in the great kitchen of the quieted farmhouse and looked out upon the listless society ebbing from the farm. Each sensed that this would be the last great debate and was reluctant to utter the words that would start their final exchange.

Digger finally spoke. "This is crazy. I've talked to everyone and no one has any idea why they are leaving or where they're going now. All anyone says is that the war is over and it's time to move on. What the hell does that mean?" he asked angrily.

"It means that something was lacking, that the Colorado Station was not home" said Jugs.

"Lacking? What are they missing here that they can find in society? Routine? Protocol? A meaningless existence clawing for prestige and wealth while all passion withers? Surely they know that what they will find in society are the very things they came here to escape," argued Boss.

"Maybe those who leave are just insincere. They came here to hide from death in war not death in society. Now that the war's over, they are taking their chances with society," Quill mused.

"Perhaps we're looking at the small arc of larger circle. Some folks have left the Station and it looks as if they are gone but maybe they have only begun a larger journey that will bring them back here again. Suppose that Jugs is right and some did feel that the Station was not quite home. Suppose that Quill is also right and some who came here were merely hiding from the war and have left because the war no longer threatens them. We know that Boss is right about the meaningless lives, which they will find in society because we know that society has not changed, only the killing has stopped. Then we also know that Digger is right because they would have to be crazy to leave the Station, which means that they will return. We are only seeing the first steps of the process, which end when they are welcomed back to the Station.

"The Station is not a refuge. It is life, Real life. The life of the human spirit. Man is a spiritual creature whose reality is love, truth, beauty, and honor. Without these, we are only sad beasts snared in triviality. The exodus will be reversed. The teepees and yurts will be full again. Think about it. Once you've seen life at the Station, can you really give it up?" insisted Cogi.

Uneasily, the compadres agreed that the disbanding residents would return. No one, they convinced themselves could really reject paradise.

Scraps of news which drifted back to the farm revealed that the departed members had made peace with the national society, and had resumed the lives, which had been disrupted by the foreign conflict. In late spring, an uncertain impetus to flee appeared to instill in the remaining farm dwellers. The shrunken gardens, the meager goods on the shelves of the food co-op, the dwindling audiences in the barn, the sense of loss, like the stench of death, impelled even reluctant members to hurriedly gather their belongings, terminate their affairs and move away from the beautiful valley. The compadres watched with alarm the disintegration of their spiritual society. One sweet clear evening in May, as the compadres sat in the kitchen looking out over their diminished domain, Cogi spoke the words that all had dreaded to utter.

"It's over. The Station is finished. We can't save it. Our friends sense that something has changed in our culture and they want to explore their lives in the midst of it. I don't know what the hell is different but I'll be leaving too."

No one argued with him; a few days later, they wished him well as he slung the great Zen bow across one shoulder, grabbed a small satchel of clothes and started down the lane towards the highway to catch a ride out of the mountains.

Within a week, Boss distributed the final orders and closed the door to the food co-op; Quill took down the stage curtains in the barn and folded them carefully and laid them on the mat in the empty meditation room; Digger cleaned the weeds from the garden, oiled the tools and hung them in the shed; and they sat down with Jugs to negotiate the formal demise of the Colorado Station.

"I think I'll stay on until the garden comes in," Jugs offered. "There's no sense in letting good food rot. I'd rather see it through and give the food to people who could really use it. And the domes, there's a lot of good building materials there and we've got tools around. I'd rather see pieces of the Station passed on, rather than abandoned."

So the potter bid his friends good-bye and with a few devoted members, remained on the farm until October. The rich produce and the tools and good lumber were distributed among the faithful just before they left. When nothing remained of the Station but his own departure, Jugs extinguished the fire in the Rex, locked the house, removed the mailbox and put it in the barn, stood briefly before the empty province, then quickly got into his truck and drove away.

Fragmented notes encircling the imprinted greetings of Christmas cards revealed the fate of the scattered compadres as they grew to middle age. After false starts in several careers, Cogi had become a real estate agent. Boss joined his father's plumbing supply business, advanced to the vice-presidency, married and produced four children. Digger rose to become the headmaster of a private school, married and sired one child. Jugs achieved fame as a potter, married, and fathered two children. Quill devoted himself to computer software, married, acquired two Volvos and remained childless.

As he took the old Zen bow down from the rafters, the real estate salesman felt a sudden flow of joy, an inexplicable delight in touching this artifact of his past. He glanced about the garage, confident that the power of the bow had vanquished his menacing daemon. He longed to polish the dusty instrument and hang it proudly above the mantle but the certainty of his wife's objections convinced him to secret his talisman in the closet in his den.

He stood in the dim light for a long time, grasping the bow and remembering, as if the wooden stick were re-charging his spirit. The quiet reverie ended with a jolting thought.

"A reunion!" he exclaimed as rushed into the house.

"I don't know," his wife said hesitantly after his lively entreaty for assistance with his plan. "I guess men embrace the past more than women do. I wish I had never gone to my high school reunion. After so many years, I should have known that it was a mistake to see my old high school friends again. Nothing is ever as satisfying it was because no one is ever the same person that they once were."

"That's right. We have all changed. But it will be great to see how Boss, Digger, Jugs, and Quill are managing the throes of middle age. Damn, I haven't seen any of them since we left the farm!"

"Doesn't that tell you something, honey?" his wife gently asked.

The real estate man did not hear her. "I know you saved their Christmas cards, so we've got the addresses. If you can just take the kids to your mother's for the day, I can get some beer and make a huge batch of lasagna. It'll be great to see those guys again."

Against her husband's excitement, she relented and sent the invitations the next morning.

On the appointed day of reunion, the land agent rousted his wife and children from bed, urged them through a hasty breakfast, and, with impatient hugs and kisses, packed them into the station wagon and waved a cursory farewell. From his closet, he then retrieved a pair of threadbare jeans, a frayed chambray shirt and worn sandals, all of which, though not worn since he abandoned the commune for a teaching position at the university, had been carefully preserved in a cedar chest. Uneasily he carried the clothes downstairs, carefully avoiding the mirror in the foyer as he rushed to the laundry room.

Hurriedly, he tossed the clothes in the washer, threw the sandals into the driveway, and hosed them furiously until the water ran clear from the soggy shoes.

With his revered clothes tumbling in the dryer and his sandals dehydrating in the brilliant sunlight, Cogi scrambled into the newly re-modeled kitchen, which, although he cooked only ceremonially, he had carefully conceived. As he plundered the many voluminous cabinets, flailed pots about wildly, chopped vegetables, and folded the dough for a huge loaf of Italian bread, Cogi was again gratified by the practical genius of his design. Sleek modern cabinets of varying size and form, each dovetailed into place according to the strictest rules of function and decor, provided ample storage for foodstuffs and cookware; appliances were positioned for optimal accessibility from each of several counters; favored pans and utensils hung conveniently upon a rack suspended from the ceiling – but the premier achievement of the arrangement had been the banishment of the kitchen table and chairs.

Just before one o'clock, the land agent shoved a loaf pan in the oven, donned his old clothes, and, as the first of his friends arrived, switched on the stereo and precisely adjusted the tonal qualities of the expensive equipment; enlivened by the lyric music, which had been one of many anthems inspiring the dwellers of Colorado Station, the land agent flung open the door to greet his guest.

"Hey, Boss, great to see you, man! Come on in," the land agent said excitedly.

"Cogi! I'm really glad it's you. I drove by several times but I wasn't sure of the address so I kept looking for a tub of beer icing down in the yard, like the old days," replied Boss uneasily.

"There's plenty in the fridge. I'll get you one. How's the plumbing business?"

"Drains the soul but fills the larder," said Boss as he marveled at the decorous foyer; trailing Cogi into the house, he added, "Snazzy digs, Cogi. You must be doing ok." As he passed through the spacious great room, Boss urgently surveyed it hoping to see the great Zen bow or the meditation rug, to catch some hint of Cogi's current metaphysic. In his pocket, carefully folded, Boss had the herbal poster, which had hung in the old kitchen. He planned to reveal the memento if the mood of the gathering became sentimental.

"I'm getting by," Cogi replied as they entered the kitchen.

Cogi took a hot loaf of bread from the oven and set it on a cooling rack; from the refrigerator he drew two bottles of beer, opened them and handed one to his guest. Once friends, now almost strangers, they faced each other uncertainly, groping for the surety of their presumed affection.

Within minutes Quill, Digger and Jugs arrived to a boisterous welcome; instinctively, the compadres gathered in the kitchen where they were bombarded with cold bottles of beer hurled from the fridge by their jubilant host.

Delivered from impending melancholy by the new arrivals, Boss greeted them with elation. "Digger! You look sharp! Those threads must have set you back plenty," he cried in admiration of his friend's dashing pin-striped suit.

Digger accepted the compliment with a weak smile barely forced through the consternation which clouded his spirit instantly as he saw that his friends were dressed casually.

Years served in the post of headmaster of an acclaimed private school had not yet supplanted his old uncertainties and Digger disconcertedly tugged at his tie in the hope of loosening it enough as to appear accidentally arranged about his neck. "I just thought you guys should see me in my professional outfit after seeing me for so many years in my grubby overalls."

"Impressive, as befits your office," remarked Jugs as he snatched a flung beer. Sensing Digger's turmoil, Jugs had spoken with customary kindness.

"Where do we light, Cogi?" Jugs continued. "There aren't any chairs in here."

"Precisely, man. I designed them out. It's not practical to have people stomping around in here when you're trying to get something done. I laid out this kitchen with a lasagna-fest in mind. When I'm charging around with pots and pans, no one entering this room would be safe anyway. Besides, man, it was a challenge to come up with a truly functional design."

"Looks like you have mastered the galley, Cogi," offered Boss.

Quill leaned against the refrigerator and surveyed the intriguing array of appliances which populated the kitchen. Characteristically, he had arrived at the reunion with no expectations, he anticipated no conclusions. "Your incredible gadgets may inspire me to fire up the old word processor and bang out a play, 'Waiting For Grubo', wherein man is mediated by the microwave," Quill said with a chuckle.

"Great," responded Cogi. "Are you still writing?"

"Only software. My Muse turned out to be non-recursive."

"I know what you mean," said Digger as Cogi led the way to the great room. Troubled that the singular formality of his dress evidenced a more profound error in his character, Digger was anxious to establish that his friends, in spite of their prior romantic venture, now led normal lives and could have easily decided to dress as he had done. "I don't feel the georgic urge that made me the cabbage king of Colorado Station. I grow a few tomatoes now, and hardly have the time to pick them."

"Hell, I get my cheese at the supermarket. These new stores have more cheeses than the old co-op ever had," Boss admitted.

"You still throwing pots?" Digger asked Jugs.

"I keep my foot to the wheel," the potter replied.

"I'm not much into yoga these days but I do resemble Buddha more closely," Cogi confessed as he tapped his slight paunch.

"Yeah, but you're really into kitchens," gibed Boss.

"Hey," responded Cogi irritably, "that renovation may have been a mundane enterprise but, before we re-modeled it, that kitchen was a lot like the old one at the farm."

"Really?" asked Digger.

"Sure," continued Cogi as he opened another beer. "Remember how big that old kitchen was? Many times, I silently crept downstairs for a midnight raid only to be foiled by the echo of the fridge door when it opened. That kitchen was a canyon."

"It must have been twenty-five feet long and fifteen feet wide," declared Digger.

"Absolutely. And the ceilings were nine feet if they were an inch," Quill said.

"And all of the cabinets and counters were on the same wall as the fridge and the cook stove. The back wall had nothing but that huge table, some chairs and that miserable old hutch," said Boss.

"What about the uneven floor? I used to get seasick just walking through the kitchen," said Cogi.

"You were taking your life in your hands if you tried to open those massive windows. The glass was held in the frames by the grease and soot from the stove but I don't know what magical force held the frames together," said Digger.

"Whatever it was, it wasn't airtight," said Quill.

"That kitchen was a real dinosaur," said Cogi.

"By now it must have fallen before the new Ice Agecondominiums," said Quill.

"Yeah. Digger's garden is probably a hot tub now," said Boss.

"I'd bet that the lake and maybe the big old oak trees in the front yard are still there," Digger suggested.

"Sure, especially the trees. Every condo complex wants its own copse on the logo to evoke a heartwarming link to the land. Man in nature. Man in condo. Homo condo," said Quill.

"Colorado Station to middle class in how many years?" asked Digger.

"Nineteen," said Jugs.

"Maybe the barn is gone and the house has been torn down but there's one thing that nobody could destroy in just nineteen years," declared Cogi.

"What?" asked Boss.

"The Rex," said Cogi.

The compadres howled at the thought of anyone trying to budge the gigantic cook stove that had presided over the old kitchen.

"That's right," said Quill. "They probably built a lovely brick terrace around it and faced the condos onto the plaza so that, while grilling steaks on their patios, the denizens could muse upon the virtues of the lost race who had forsaken the black iron reliquary."

"What a mountain that stove was! It took a cord of wood to fill the firebox," said Digger.

"Yes, but when you come downstairs on a cold winter morning, fire it up, get a pot of coffee brewing and shove some Danish rolls in the warming ovens, it is magnificent," said Jugs.

"What about that enormous kitchen table? We did everything on that table – clean a kilo of weed, make kites, sew buttons," said Cogi emphatically.

"Sprout beans, make candles," Digger added.

"Make posters, print radical propaganda," Quill interjected.

"Fix stereos," Boss remembered aloud.

"Bake bread," Digger contributed unconsciously as he too was moved by memory.

"Eat," said Quill.

"Drink," said Boss.

"Argue," said Cogi.

"Discuss, not argue," Jugs.

"You call ranting and raving, discussion?" asked Cogi.

"Yes. Truth, beauty, and meaning engaged in mortal combat with lies and ugliness and emptiness: we were the champions of the passionate life. Remember?" challenged Jugs.

"Who won?" quipped Quill.

"Let's look it up in the encyclopedia!" cried Boss.

"Hell yes! We always did that," said Digger.

"We spent half our time just searching through those books," said Boss.

"I think we must have worn out the pages on classical civilization, science, and philosophy," said Cogi.

"I'll bet we learned more ripping through those Britannicas than we ever did in class. By rights, our tuition belongs to Jugs. Those books were his," said Boss.

"Pay up! I could use the money," Jugs said with a knowing chuckle.

"Remember when Boss hit the chapter on astronomy? Then he had to pore over the sections on cosmology, the ancient Greeks, and mythology – we spent every night that summer sprawled on the grass by the lake gazing at the heavens, trying to take the measure of man in the universe," said Quill, suddenly inspired by the past again.

"And agonizing over the ends of the good life," said Boss, now recalling a familiar and pleasing version of himself.

"Then there were the great literary debates. The vision of the Russian masters versus the towering genius of our Southern writers. Tolstoy triumphs over Southern gothic," said Cogi, now conjuring the spirited discussions of spirit.

"Don't forget the countless readings of dark and obscure poetry," added Quill.

"I remember one time when Cogi had just discovered Plato and Boss was heavy into Nietzsche. Damn! What a battle that was!" exclaimed Digger, relaxing in recollection of that furious argument which had drawn his attention away from the personal doubts that tormented him.

"Everybody got pulled into that one. Jugs almost kicked the leg off of the table when Quill said that Sartre didn't know shit from Spinoza," said Boss with a laugh.

Quill said tauntingly, "I was right."

"Not true," Jugs rejoined, "there's more to nothing than meets the eye."

"Hey, let's don't start that again. This is not the farm. We're not wrestling with nothingness anymore," Cogi objected with a frosty voice intended to quell the brewing discussion.

"How can you tell?" Quill asked his disapproving host.

"Very funny," Digger retorted harshly. "Philosophy doesn't pay the bills. Whatever else it may have been, the farm was definitely a refuge from reality."

"Exactly, that's why we all eventually moved out. A person needs tangible, productive goals and realistic values," said Cogi.

"That's true. I don't have the time to write anymore," Quill said harmoniously, flashing an amicable smile at Digger, "but I still enjoy literature."

"Sure," said Cogi, "and I still dig great music, especially when the sounds are piped through a decent audio system."

"I'm positive that we all appreciate the peace that came with the end of that damned war," said Boss.

"Absolutely," concurred Digger. "And we're still doing essentially the same things as we did on the farm. Boss is still managing commerce--granted, honey and cheese were more romantic than valves and toilets but he's filling orders just the same. Cogi peddles paradise, as always. I'm cultivating minds instead of cabbages. Jugs throws pots. Quill writes software rather than fiction."

"Wait a minute," Quill objected. Some of my programs could truthfully be called fiction."

"The farm was a great place in its day," argued Cogi. "You can't deny that it engendered a mythic ethos, spurred us to the pursuit of ideals—but we didn't really penetrate reality until we began to function in it. Not in dreams, but in the actual forces, the limiting conditions of life. Negotiating the pressures of jobs and marriages and kids and mortgages and tax shelters, that is the real challenge. Good Scotch and ski weekends are the things that rejuvenate the soul. The farm was the province of truth but it sure as hell lacked operational validity. Right down to the kitchen. What a dinosaur! You wouldn't want to live like that now. Space must be functional. Resources must be utilized intelligently," he said vehemently. "Tolstoy and the practical kitchen. Of these, only a practical kitchen increases the resale value of a house."

"You really did a great job on your kitchen, Cogi. How about taking a look at mine sometime?" asked Boss.

"Sure."

"Ours is a cramped, ugly little room," said Quill.

"I've got a wreck. It's a miracle that we can even cook a meal in it," Digger complained. Jugs remained silent.

"Come on Jugs, out with it," Quill insisted, "tell us about your wretched galley."

"I'd have to call it Early Jurassic," replied Jugs.

His friends roared with laughter as each imagined a drab, awful, hopelessly inadequate room.

"About six years ago, I bought the farm," Jugs announced with a proud grin. "I even found the old mailbox in the attic and nailed it back on the Judas tree. The Colorado Station lives!"

His friends were astounded.

"Far out!" cried Boss.

"Congratulations," said Quill provisionally.

"Unbelievable," proclaimed Cogi.

"Have you kept the garden?" Digger asked glumly, as a ribbon of anguish deftly coiled itself around his recently bright spirit: if the garden had been abandoned, then the esteem accorded him for his prior cultivation would be debased by the present irrelevance of his feat; if, however, the garden endured under the auspices of the new steward, then, to the extent that it now flourished, his achievement would be also diminished.

"I only have time enough away from the kiln to manage a small part of your old plot. I keep a little patch of corn in the field but most of the land is fallow, awaiting the sure hand of a compadre. Come on out, all of you. Put in a crop," offered Jugs.

"How fares the lake?" asked Quill.

"I had a whale of a time clearing the springs but now the water runs sweet and clear. The gazebo collapsed during an ice storm. We could build another one and stage our famous sunset concerts by the lake. I know we can still play the golden music," Jugs answered enthusiastically.

"Is the barn standing?" asked Boss.

"Solidly. In fact, the tack room looks like you just left. Dust off the shelves and the co-op could be back in business tomorrow," cried Jugs.

"What about the house?" Cogi inquired.

"It needs a new roof, badly. I replaced a lot of rotten wood and painted the house, inside and out. The Rex is still enthroned in the kitchen."

"It must be great to be back at the Station, you know, like you never even left," Boss said enviously.

"Yes," agreed Jugs, "but I did leave and the return was not easy. There was so much work to do just to save the place, and so many beautiful memories to justify the effort, that I didn't realize for quite some time how hard it would be to live in paradise. During the first winter, a furious snowstorm buried the farm. Fields and fences, the garden path, the frozen lake, the springhouse—the landmarks of the Colorado Station were lost beneath the deep drifts. Indistinguishable in the unbroken snow, the farm looked foreign and uninviting. Even the barn seemed strange, looming starkly above the avalanche with the desolation of an empty Laundromat. It was incredible that a simple layer of snow could erase understanding yet, as I stood at the kitchen window, I could not comprehend the farm, could not feel what it meant, could not be moved by Colorado Station. Then I remembered the first time I had ever stood in that kitchen, the pledge I had made to make the farm a place for the spirit; and I recalled the temper of the life that was lived there, the beauty and passion of it. The scape of the spirit, not the land, that is what I had come back for. And that would be the hardest to restore. I stoked up the Rex, put on some hot chocolate, quaffed a piping mug then struggled out to the barn, hauled the Britannicas down from the loft, dragged them into the kitchen and put them back on the hutch. Since then, I've found a few chapters we still need to cover."

As the potter happily recounted his plans to expand the garden and rebuild the gazebo, his fellow compadres repeatedly expressed their amazement that Jugs had acquired the old farm and still lived in the manner of its romance.

Elated by the potter's keen entreaty for a reformation of the old league, the beseeched friends savored remembrances of the eminent society of the Colorado Station; then, realizing that the potter's suit was unanswered, they cautiously eyed one another, hoping that one would break their irresolute ranks. None accepted the potter's charge. Like flowers upon a windowsill, they bloomed now upon the surface of life, warmed and watered on a stable ledge; their roots were tightly wound within the pot, unable to break free yet still inclined towards the middle earth if ever they should fall to the ground.

The reunion drew to an early end when Digger, wracked with volatile uncertainties in the face of the old creed, rose to leave; he was immediately joined by Quill, who mused on the awesome inertia, which lay between the present and some future resumption of the spirited life of the farm. Boss lingered for a moment, absorbed in the belated comprehension that his notion of reality was strictly associative, borrowed from peers, and that his marriage had endowed his current society with a permanence from which he would not likely escape. Passing Jugs as he headed for the door, Boss offered him the herbal poster and asked that it be restored to its rightful place in the kitchen.

"Keep it, Boss. You can put it back yourself when you come out to the farm," Jugs said in refusal.

When his guests had departed, Cogi quickly cleaned the kitchen and switched off the light. In the instant, the room fell into darkness and his eyes struggled to accept the fled brightness, Cogi's daemon appeared and hauntingly dissolved into a clear image of the old farm kitchen, laden with produce, cluttered with the artifacts of inquiry, ringing with the songs of spirited hearts. As the icon slowly faded, the dream merchant was struck by the hard cold bite of the paradise hook.

THE END

The Humanoids are Coming
Ian Fletcher

Robots are going to replace us and there is nothing we can do about it. One reason, it's already too late. Many industrial jobs are already done by robots. Their quality is better. They don't come in hung over. They work 24-hour shifts.

In 1988, a consulting firm advised Kodak to forget film. The future was digital. Get on the bandwagon early. Kodak fired them.

Now here's the prediction that no one wants to believe: robots are coming. We will be merging, mating, and morphing with them. We're already becoming mechanized. Knee and hip replacements. A Google contact lens that measures our blood sugar. The Swedish fingertip chip that lets employees unlock the office and fire up the copier.

A Spanish cancer survivor has received the first 3D-printed titanium chest prosthetic In a few years we'll have people walking among us who are partially – perhaps mostly – 3D-printed.

Scientists are developing prosthetics controlled by our minds, not muscle. At Johns Hopkins hospital, a double arm-amputee can think, "I'd like a sip of that coffee," and his augmented body responds. People with bone and muscle diseases benefit from lab-made limbs today. One day we might tell our body to fly home. Or to grandma's.

The Royal Melbourne Institute of Technology, researchers have created an electronic memory cell. A bionic brain will soon be here, and who wouldn't want a Boost, something to crank up our memory? Then pass what it knows on to our children.

There's a wireless brain implant, the size of a grain of rice, which Stanford researchers say can get rid of a bad mood? We could sign up for a jolt of optimism.

What about multi-billion-dollar pharmaceutical industry that makes all those happy drugs Lexapro, Paxil, Zoloft, and Prozac? They will disappear as quickly as a mood swing.

Here's where I think we ought to worry. We're not dealing with mechanized body parts. We're re-engineering our minds, our spirit, our souls. We go from robot knees to robot brains. The robot brain will be smarter that the one you were born with. Think about it. Your new brain won't have to learn anything. New skills and knowledge will simply be uploaded in a millisecond. Or less.

We can adjust, or be left in the dust. It's not just we humans, who are evolving. Our automatons are, too.

Some are already here for us to see. Bots with cute names like, Echo, Jibo, Nao, and Pepper, are ready to march into our homes to help our kids with homework and bedtime stories. In Japan, robotic caregivers tend to the elderly and play concierge at deluxe hotels. The technology can be used to develop into sex robots. You can buy a perfectly matched partner who knows, and agrees to, your every desire.

There's a huge melting pot up ahead. Humans being enhanced by technology. Robots infused with human personalities. Breeding with each other??? New DNA. The transformation of our species is on the way, and 2016 is when the average person slowly awakens to the new dawn of Robo Humanity.

The Swiss have developed altruistic and deceitful robots. Who in the heck needs that!

Things I Learned Living in the South
Unknown Source

- A possum is a flat animal that sleeps in the middle of the road.
- There are 5,000 types of snakes and 4,998 of them live in the South.
- There are 10,000 types of spiders. All 10,000 of them live in the South, plus a couple no one's seen before.
- If it grows, it'll stick ya. If it crawls, it'll bite cha.
- Onced and Twiced are words.
- It is not a shopping cart, it is a buggy!
- Jawl-P? means, Did you all go to the bathroom?
- Fixinto is one word. It means I'm going to do that.
- There is no such thing as lunch. There is only dinner and then there's supper.
- Iced tea is appropriate for all meals and you start drinking it when you're two.
- Backwards and forwards means I know everything about you.
- The word jeet is actually a question meaning, 'Did you eat?'
- You don't have to wear a watch, because it doesn't matter what time it is, you work until you're done or it's too dark to see.
- You don't PUSH buttons, you MASH em.
- Ya'll is singular. All ya'll is plural.
- All the festivals across the state are named after a fruit, vegetable, grain, insect, or animal.
- You carry jumper cables in your car – for your OWN car.
- You only own five spices: salt, pepper, mustard, Tabasco and ketchup.
- Everyone you meet is a Honey, Sugar, Miss(first name) or Mr.(first name)
- You think that the first day of deer season is a national holiday.
- You know what a hissy fit is.
- Fried catfish is the other white meat.
- We don't need no dang Driver's Ed. If our mama says we can drive, we can drive!!!

Contributors

P.L. Almanza: *From the Kitchen of P. L. Almanza*; lives in Hamlet, North Carolina. She has been writing stories since she was four years old. Her first book, *The East Side Killers* came out in April 2014. Her cookbook, *Family Meals and Desserts*, came out in the summer of 2015. She is currently working on Cat Tales.

E. B. Alston: Author, columnist, literary critic, and sometimes poet. His work has been published in various newspapers, telecommunications trade magazines, and books. He is the Managing Editor of the magazine.

Elizabeth Silance Ballard: *Life With Elizabeth;* is a magazine columnist and author of *Three Letters from Teddy and Other Stories*, co-author of *Whoopin and Hollerin in Onslow County, Kate's Fan, Christmas Without Koyoko, The Fourth Wife of A Markham Gillespie*, and *Welcome Home, Teddy Stallard.* Elizabeth is also editor of *The Tar Heel Star News*.

Rita Berman: *The SS United States of America;* was born in London, England, is a free-lance writer, lecturer, editor, and author of *Still Hopping, Still Hoping*, the biography of Carla Shuford, (2012), and *The A - Z of Writing and Selling,* a Writer's Digest Book Club selection Sept, 1981. Her work has appeared in more than 500 travel, feature, business, and trade journal articles, as well as newspaper columns for diverse publications in the United States and Great Britain. Her books are *Dating Adventures of a Widow* Her latest book, *The Key,* came out in 2013.

Randy Bittle: *Why the Greeks?;* is an independent philosopher living in Raleigh and currently working on a beginner's book about modern philosophy.

Peggy Ellis: *Who Was Franklin Delano Roosevelt;* is a writer and editor who resides in Black Mountain, NC.

Ian Fletcher: *The Humanoids are Coming;* Retired mechanical engineer. This is his first article for the magazine.

Diana Goldsmith: *Ann's Story;* is a retired teacher in England. She lives in Chard, Somerset.

Joan Leotta: *Appetite for Mulberries, Crocus Dreams and Mother's Day Thanks;* has been writing and performing since childhood. Calabash Headline: *Local Author has Hat Trick Summer—three books!* Three of this Calabash, NC award winning journalist and performer's books have been released this summer. Moreover, each book is in a different genre! One is romance/women's fiction, the second is a collection of short stories, and the third is Joan Leotta's first picture book.

Ariana Mangum: *A Mrs. Haunch's Last Appearance;* is a retired English teacher and author of *When the Goldenrod Sang in the Meadows, A Forgotten Landscape and Where the Butterflies Roam*. Her newest book, *Shenandoah Promise, is* out.

John Hamilton McWhorter V: *English is Not Normal* is an American academic, political commentator, and linguist, professor at Columbia University where he teaches linguistics, American studies, philosophy, and music history.

Carol Leigh Alston Rados: *A Story from My Youth in Essex, North Carolina;* graduated from East Carolina University and got a job with North Carolina Social Services. She retired at the end of 2015 after over 40 years and has written a story for publication!

Leigh Jean Russell: *Why Can't Women be Assertive and Men be Feisty;* Lives in Faison, North Carolina, is a retired school teacher, who taught English. The editor met her several years ago when he was writing a series on the towns on Highway 50, between Creedmoor, NC and Topsail Beach, NC. Mrs. Russell said over lunch that Faison High School was so small that they taught driving and sex education in the same automobile. This is her first published work.

Sybil Austin Skakle: *A Surprising Bargain*; grew up in Hatteras, NC, born January 10, 1926, was a hospital pharmacist for 23 years, has published poetry, *Searchings*, 2001; a memoir, *Confessions of an Outer Banks Filly*, 2002; another memoir *Valley of the Shadow*, 2009. Her work has appeared in periodicals and numerous poetry and prose anthologies, four of which were published by The Chapel Hill Writers' Discussion Group. She has been a member of Friday Noon Poets for more than thirty years.

Michael Warren: *Tolstoy and the Practical Kitchen;* is the author of the novel *The Estrangement of the Rain God*, 2nd edition, published by Righter Books. He maintains his author web site at http//:www.tiliks.com. His first novel is the first of a teratology, *The Glory River Saga*. He has just completed the second novel, *The Cripple Goat*. His newest book, a children's book, *Squeach and the Magical Starfish* came out in 2015.

Dave Whitford: *How Things Change;* writes from retirement in Toano, Virginia, after a labor lifetime that included kitchen scullery, soda jerking, radar maintenance, boat and marine-engine sales and repair, technical writing, wedding photography, golf-course maintenance, metal fabrication, and house construction and inspection.

Marry Williamson: *A New Year at Sunset Lodge;* lives in Chard, Somerset, England. She was born in the Netherlands and moved to Britain in 1966. She worked for an Anglo-Dutch company in London. In 1999, Marry and her husband retired and moved to Chard, Somerset. Her hobbies are writing, reading, bird watching, and exploring ancient monuments. She is a member of a local writers' group in England.

Tim Whealton: *A Day in the Gunshop,* review of *Dove Hunting and Shotgunning* and *Starting Over;* writes a regular column from New Bern, NC. He is a gunsmith whose shop is in Cove City, North Carolina. His book, *According to Tim* was published last year.

"I would that you all to me,
You that are so much to me, no more.
I pluck the rose
And love it more than tongue can speak

Then the good minute goes."

Robert Browning (1812-1899)

Righter Quarterly Review – Spring 2016

Printed and bound in the United States of America by E. B. Alston.
Copyright 2016

ISBN 978-1-938527-33-3

Corporate Offices
1112 Rogers Road
Graham, NC 27253

Telephone: 336-525-1520
Email: righterpub@esinc.net

Print copies available on Amazon. The Electronic version is available from Amazon Kindle-Free
to Prime Members